The Musicians

Profit Path:

The 5-Stage Blueprint
to Produce Massive Growth
in Your Fan Base
andSustainable Income
forYour Music Career

by *Bree Noble*

Copyright © 2019 Bree Noble

CLAIM YOUR FREE GIFT

19 Proven Sources of Income You Probably Haven't Considered For Your Music Career

Uncover 19 hidden streams of income to transform your career **from "starving artist" to profitable professional musician**.

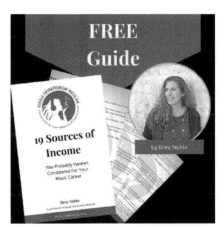

✓ A real-world, 19-point game plan that takes the guesswork out of turning your passion and creativity into dollars

✓ 5 strategies you can apply right now to start making money from music (even if you're a beginner)

✓ 2 little-known income sources only open to female artists

Visit http://femusician.com/income to claim your free gift.

Table of Contents

Acknowledgements

I want to thank my husband, Chris, and my two girls, Julia and Abigail, for giving me the space and encouragement to write this book. Thank you to Jill and Josh Stanton for developing their *"Momentum Marketing"* system which inspired **The Musician's Profit Path** framework. Thank you to Sara Christiansen, Kelly Christian and Rebecca Undem for their input on the framework and for helping me come up with the title, ***"The Musician's Profit Path"***. Finally, thank you to the members of the Female Musician Academy who have implemented this path and inspire me every day to continue helping musicians to build solid businesses using this 5-stage blueprint.

Introduction

The music business has changed a *lot* in the last 15 years. Technology has opened up so many opportunities to Indie Artists, introducing a whole new breed of "overnight success stories" who have had a video go viral and suddenly, they are the next big thing.

But for every one of these, there are hundreds of thousands of musicians trying to build a following online and offline so they can become a professional musician who makes a steady living from music. I'm not going to mislead you. There is a *lot* of competition out there because technology has opened up the playing field for just about any artist who wants to share their talent (or lack of talent) with the world.

That's the bad news. But the good news for you is that the majority of Indie Artists out there don't know the right way to build a music career.

Because you're reading this, you will learn how to build it right from the beginning and have the upper hand on your competition. Most musicians don't know how to systematically build their fan base from the ground up to create a sustainable income from music so they can become a full-time, professional musician.

Instead, many artists spend all their time and energy (and often money) trying to get the attention of Music Industry "decision-makers" at record labels who they think hold the key to their future. They try various tactics, grasping at straws, hoping to get "discovered". They don't understand that the *new* music business doesn't work that way anymore. I get it, because I did exactly that for almost 10 years.

I wanted so badly to escape my 9-to-5 job as a Director of Finance. I wanted to exchange the hum-drum drudgery of an office job for an exciting, passion-driven career as a professional musician, but I didn't even know how to start. I spent a ton of time and money doing all the wrong things, only to end up frustrated and back at square one.

However, you're different because you have the opportunity to learn from my mistakes and start off on the right foot, taking the right path from the beginning to build a lasting career, step-by-step, from the ground up.

This blueprint is called *The Musician's Profit Path* because it's a step-by-step, long-range plan for any unknown Indie Artist to build a solid, sustainable and profitable music career.

This book will outline the steps for you to discover and then follow — to go from unknown Indie Artist to a profitable, professional musician.

You see, I built this blueprint because I too, like many artists, did everything backwards and wasted tons of time and money following rabbit trails that would never pay off. I watched other successful musicians and tried to duplicate their results. There can be some merit to this strategy, but I didn't have the complete picture. I didn't realize that those musicians were several stages ahead of me in their career, so trying to apply the strategies they were using wouldn't work for me because I hadn't laid the groundwork first.

It would be like trying out for a major league baseball team without even playing in the minor leagues, or even learning the fundamentals in Little League. You can't expect to cut to the front of the line. You have to put in the time and pay your dues.

But there is a strategic way to do it that reduces confusion and increases your chance of success. That's why I created *The Musician's Profit Path*.

This blueprint is the strategic plan I would employ if I started my music career today, knowing everything I know now – including valuable lessons learned from making tons of mistakes along the way.

Having a blueprint to follow is extremely important. These days, there is more online information than ever about how to build a music career. The problem is that it's disjointed, incomplete and often outdated.

Often, the reason students join my Academy or take my courses is that they've tried to do their own research by reading countless blogposts, listening to advice on podcasts and following what they see other musicians doing. This creates a "deer in the headlights" effect. They're on information overload. They don't know what to do first, and without any clear goals and established mission or direction, they are lost. Feeling overwhelmed kills their motivation and they end up doing nothing.

I don't want that to happen to you! I know you're a talented, passionate musician with a great deal to offer the world through your music. I created *The Musician's Profit Path* so you always know the next step to take in order to move forward.

9

You can move as quickly through the stages as your time and energy allows. Some of my students have enthusiastically conquered all the hurdles in **Stage 1** in just one to two months. Others only have a few hours per week to devote to music, so **Stage 1** can take three to six months.

How quickly you move through the stages is up to you. Most importantly, this blueprint gives you the assurance that the time and money you spend on music is being spent wisely. It also puts you in the driver's seat. Finally, you'll have the knowledge and tools that really work to build your own career with no need for a manager, a label or a booking agent. You are in control. You can make it happen.

If you follow the blueprint, you'll be leaps and bounds ahead of other artists who don't have a plan (more on that later). As my student Wanda said, "This framework taught me how to focus on the right things and stop doing things that weren't valuable to my career."

We often refer to ourselves as DIY (Do It Yourself) musicians. As Indies, we have to do a lot of the work ourselves to make progress but that doesn't mean we have to learn it all firsthand ourselves through trial and error. *The Musician's Profit Path* is a shortcut.

Following *The Musician's Profit Path* cuts your learning curve considerably, so you can spend less time learning and more time doing. If I'd had this blueprint when I first started, I would not have spent 10 years wasting time and money on things that didn't work.

I know from experience that if you follow the steps in **The Musician's Profit Path**, you'll cut years off of your journey from unknown Indie Artist to profitable, Professional Musician.

Before you dive into the blueprint, I'll help you figure out which stage you are currently in, so you'll know where to start. No matter which stage you are in now, you'll want to review the previous stages to make sure you go back and fill any holes. Having a solid foundation in place will make every step along the path easier.

Most importantly, no matter what stage you're in now, even if you're at ground zero, don't be intimidated by the 5 stages. Keep in mind that progression through the stages can take anywhere from one to five years. How fast you progress is a function of several factors: time, energy, talent, focus, relationships and even luck.

Don't feel as if you have to do everything in this book right away. This is a long-range plan, but, don't let that keep you from getting started right now!

The best way to use this book is to read it all the way through so you can get a big picture of the career path and the progression you'll be following through the 5 stages.

Once you've gotten a good overview, go to the section for the stage that best describes where you are now. Take the assessment at the beginning to see if you've reached all the benchmarks. If you're missing a few, go back to the previous stage and work on those first. Once you've knocked those out, go back and start working through the tasks in your current stage.

Are you ready to get started on your *Musician's Profit Path* journey?

Great! But first, let's lay a little ground work.

The Rules of The New Music Industry

In the old music business, inking a record deal was the holy grail. In fact, it was almost exclusively the only way to make it as an artist. This was a huge barrier to entry for unknown Indies.

Nowadays, that barrier has been removed. There are loads of successful unsigned artists making a living from music, hitting the radio and record charts, and touring the world. The playing field has rapidly expanded, and with it, come massive opportunities for artists.

But the Music Industry "establishment" still wants you to think you need *them* to get started – that you are *powerless* without them. Nonsense!

You are a thriving, creative, wonderful artist (no matter your age, by the way). You are passionate, smart and dedicated. You have everything you need to create a successful music career on your own. Well, almost everything.

The knowledge to succeed is right here within your grasp. It is what will give you the upper hand, the POWER over the music industry's lies that you need <u>them</u> to have a sustainable career in music.

How do you do it? You can establish your own <u>real</u> business – a solid foundation with your brand, instead of leaving your fate to the mercy of record executives who might decide you're not young enough, not "sexy" enough, not "commercial" or not "relevant".

Who needs that?! There is a perfect audience for your music, hungry to hear and purchase your creative output, just waiting for you to find them.

I don't care if you're 16 or 66. If you make great music, there are people out there who want to hear it and support you by purchasing it, attend your live shows and be your champion online and offline.

That's what **The Musician's Profit Path Blueprint** can do for you.

Skeptical? I don't blame you, but I have worked with women of all ages and genres who have followed this.

How do the labels fit into this new music economy? In the *new* music business, the record labels don't have budgets like they used to have for developing new talent. They are looking for artists who have already honed their craft and built a sizable following online and offline.

So, whether you decide to eventually get signed to a label or not, you still have to do the hard work to build a fan base, which is why this 5-Stage blueprint is so valuable.

Music Industry Lies: Don't Let Them Hold You Back

I can't tell you how often I hear musicians getting bad advice and feedback about how the music industry works. I just want to scream, "Wait! No! Don't listen to that. It's just not true! I'm proof that you can do it, despite the challenges!"

The big problem is that the people who are the so-called "Industry Experts" giving the advice have a completely one-sided view of the Industry. They proclaim youth and physical appearance as the be-all of success in the industry.

Yes, back when the labels held all the power, this was the case. Labels spent a lot of money to develop artists, so they needed to be as confident as possible that their new artist would succeed. One way to do that, especially in this video-saturated generation, was to invest in artists with youth and looks because that had proven to sell records.

The record execs look at the world chiefly from the "bottom line" perspective. They only have so much money to invest, so they have to pick sure-fire winners. I have been a Director of Finance for an opera company, so I understand their perspective and I really can't blame them.

So, what about those of us who don't fit this mold? Some of us, like me, have a "mom tummy" that we can't seem to eradicate no matter how many sit-ups we do, and the idea of "shakin' it" on camera is laughable.

What about age? Many of my students have been told that after 30 they may as well pack it in because there are no opportunities for them in music. WHAT? It took me 10 years after graduating from college to actually figure this stuff out. By then, I was 32. That's when I recorded my first studio album.

I had my biggest touring and income year when I was pregnant with my second daughter. But by then, I had built a reputation based upon my talent, my songs and my personality. No one cared that I was wearing maternity clothes.

I have students who have jumped back into the game after taking a break for various reasons: corporate careers, raising kids, etc. Now they are making consistent money from music.

Age ain't nothin' but a number! Your talent and passion will outshine all the ravages of time, I promise. Your perfect audience is out there, and they don't care that you're not 25 and beautiful. They'd rather benefit from the wealth of experience and wisdom you've gathered that only comes with age.

My students and I didn't listen to the pervasive lies that youth and looks are what matter. We forged our own path – and you can too. You are talented, passionate musicians with a message to share with the world. There is a place for that message in the music business. It just won't look like the traditional label route. You can carve out your own niche, and that's what *The Musician's Profit Path* framework is all about.

In this era of the music industry, WE have the power to make it happen for ourselves, and we don't have to wait around either. We can do it right now!

When we find our niche and build our fan base, the labels won't be able to dispute our value. As I said before, labels need to invest in sure-fire winners, and having already built a fan base makes you extremely attractive to labels.

The question is, after you do the hard work to grow your following and build a career for yourself, will you even care about attracting a label anymore?

Don't Be A Lone Ranger

I want to bring to light something that I know plagues Indie artists, especially female artists – something that not many people want to talk about, and something that you are probably feeling right now or have felt in the past:

Loneliness.

Isolation.

Fear.

I know all about these crippling emotions. I felt them every day for 10 years when I thought about my music career. They made me feel like giving up.

I felt lost! But then, I went to an event and met an artist who was performing the kind of gigs I wanted to perform, who had a solid presence online and had built a real fan base.

Of course, I was jealous! But instead of succumbing to the green-eyed monster, I decided to befriend her and try to "pick her brain."

Luckily, she was very gracious and generous with her time and advice. Not only that, but she had started a group of like-minded musicians just for female artists and she invited me to join. I felt like I had hit the jackpot! In terms of my future career growth, I had.

I jumped into the group discussion with both feet. I learned everything I could from the women there.

They all had such diverse backgrounds and experiences to learn from. Even though I thought the members might be territorial and competitive, they were all so helpful, giving and kind. None of them were stingy with their knowledge or their time.

Why was this the case? Because the founders of the group created a culture of generosity, reciprocity and "paying it forward." Everyone had an "abundance" mindset. They felt there were enough gigs, fans and sales for everyone.

They were genuinely interested in the promotion and success of all Indie artists because they believed that "all boats rise with the tide" and "rise" I did.

I can trace most of my success as an Indie artist back to being a part of that group for several years. Spending just 30 minutes per day talking with the women in the group gave me the confidence, know-how and energy to build my career from scratch.

The biggest benefit from joining the group was that I was no longer alone, isolated and afraid. I was part of a group of women who had become like sisters to me (as close as sisters can be, never having met in person). They gave me pep talks, guided me through the ugliness, and celebrated with me when I hit milestones.

It was magical, and without that group I probably would have given up years ago. So now, 10 years later, I decided to "pay it forward" and create a similar community.

My *Female Indie Musician Community* is an online group with a nurturing atmosphere of like-minded women, putting their collective heads together and sharing knowledge and experience for the greater good of us all. If you're a female artist, you can join us here in the <u>Female Indie Musician Community</u>.

Whether you join my community or not, I implore you to find a community of like-minded musicians and get involved. In person or online, gender-specific or genre-specific, find a collective that's a good fit for you, where you'll receive solid support.

Embrace Your Uniqueness and Find Your Niche

As a musician, I've had quite a diverse background. In high school, I sang with Madrigal groups, performed in classical solo competitions and participated in a major performance of a Christian concert at a Marine base. I was even the lead in a women's Sweet Adeline-style quartet (gotta dig up a picture of us in our hobo outfits singing *"Side by Side"*!)

In college, I studied classical voice and opera (I am a lyric soprano). I sang a lead role in *The Marriage of Figaro*, while simultaneously performing in a touring group that performed positive pop/rock (with a full band) and a cappella arrangements. That's where I cut my teeth as a performer.

After college, for the first 10 years of my career, I was a paid soloist for Vivaldi's "Gloria" and Mozart's "Mass In C Major," sang Shania Twain and LeeAnn Rimes songs at weddings and rocked out as lead vocalist for a band that played Green Day, Lauren Hill and Vertical Horizon.

So, was I a Classical Diva, a Country Karaoke Queen, or a Rocker Chick? Your guess is as good as mine. We're talking Identity Crisis!

Because I had such a wide range of abilities and diverse interests, I could perform in many different styles or musical arrangements. Was this a good thing? Yes and no.

Since I *could* do all these things, I *did* do ALL of them. It was fun and it was challenging, but it was confusing. What did I want to *be* when I grew up, or rather, grew into my *identity* as an artist? I had no clue.

All of my confusion, identity-crisis angst and lack of direction came to a head when I was about 30.

I had joined a female Alternative Pop/Rock band (that's right, another *new* style I had not explored) called Not Martha. I sang lead in a vocal style that was NOT me, very imitative, derivative of early 2000s Alternative Pop/Rock bands like The Calling, Creed, Collective Soul and Fuel.

WAIT! A classical lyric soprano singing Third Eye Blind and The Goo Goo Dolls? How does that work? I pulled it off, but it WASN'T me.

However, the founder had big dreams, big plans and seemed to have the drive to get us somewhere. I adapted my style, my persona and my career desire to match hers, all in the name of "making it."

I knew I was outside of my comfort zone, but not the kind of uncomfortable feeling you get when you know you're doing the right thing, but you're afraid to do it. It was the kind where you know you're doing the wrong thing, but you've convinced yourself you should do it anyway.

Just look at this picture I resurrected from the archives.

Who walks down a suburban street carrying a keyboard? Just saying!

Was any of this branding "me"? Absolutely not! I don't even like wearing sunglasses. And I'd never carry my keyboard around that way. I have a large case with wheels (the only way to go)!

But, I played along because I wanted a music career, and I thought this was the "magic bullet" for me.

We had been playing gigs around Orange County, and finally landed a pretty lucrative show at a good-sized venue.

I was excited about this major performance! I was READY. I told everyone about it. I just knew this was the beginning of something big – and then I got on stage.

It was like I was inside of a dream, watching myself perform. I think back to it now, and it still feels that way. It was like watching some other band on TV performing. I thought, who is that girl trying to be something she's not?

When it was over, I didn't even acknowledge all the accolades, the congratulations and the "high fives." They didn't even register because it was like they were for somebody else, and in a sense, they were.

At that moment, I knew I'd never succeed as a part of Not Martha, not because we didn't have the talent and the drive to make it, but because I could never put my whole heart into something that was clearly *someone else's dream*.

That major performance was the beginning of the end for Not Martha. It ended as badly as bands often do for the common reasons that they end – musical differences, lack of a shared vision and values, and lack of a unified commitment.

Before that gig, I was "all in," but for the wrong reasons. That experience was the turning point for my career because I realized I needed to find a direction for my career where I could be "all in" and not feel like a fraud.

So, I embarked on the journey to find my "musical self." It took some real soul searching, some deep thinking, and then, a lot of self-examination.

Who was I REALLY as an artist?

What did I REALLY want from my music career?

Once I got real with myself and wrote it all down on paper, then, and only then, could I start to craft a plan to take me there.

Why Indie Artists Need a Plan

Artists who understand the rules of the new music business usually fall into a different trap. They try to copy all of the different tactics they see successful artists using.

Most of the time, this doesn't work. Strategies that work for artists who have already had some success won't work for beginners. They just aren't effective.

Even worse, unknown artists spend lots of money on Public Relations (PR) agents and radio promoters when they haven't yet put their foundational pieces together, such as a musician website and a social media following. This "cart before the horse" scenario is like trying to sell a house before you've even laid a single brick.

I hate to see artists waste their money like this! Don't get me wrong – PR and radio campaigns can be very useful for those in a later stage of their career, but I definitely don't recommend them for artists in the early stages of career growth. Save your money. I suggest not even thinking about that kind of investment until you reach Stage 4.

To save you money, time, headaches and heartache, I've created a **5-Stage Blueprint** for building a solid foundation. Then, you can add the right bricks at the right time to construct an unshakable, profitable music career as a professional musician.

The five stages take you from Foundation to Profession in a step-by-step format so you know *what* to focus on and *when* (and what *not* to focus on!).

This framework provides you with clear marching orders, but how do you make sure you make steady progress without taking on too much? I know that there's a temptation for musicians who follow the profit path to pile their plate as high as possible with tasks so they can move faster and make it to the next stage.

As DIY artists, we are hustlers, and we've gotten far with the hustler mentality. However, I want to strongly warn you against long-term hustle. It can lead to burnout (see Stage 3) or complete abandonment of music. I know right now you're probably full of enthusiasm and think this could never happen, but trust me, continuous hustling can wear down even the most zealous Indies.

Instead, I encourage you to work in 90-day sprints.

> ➤ Pick five goals from the list of benchmarks on the checklist at the end of each stage.

> ➤ Next, write down a list of smaller action steps and bite-sized tasks discussed in the book that you can work on daily, or weekly, to make progress toward achieving those five goals.

> ➤ Schedule a check-in meeting with yourself at the end of each week to see how you're progressing. Give yourself a virtual high five for the items you've completed. Don't beat yourself up if you didn't finish as much as you wanted. Just think through the obstacles you

encountered that kept you from finishing that goal, and brainstorm about how you can avoid them next week.

➢ Rinse and repeat for the next week, pulling forward any items that didn't get completed or need more work. Add new items in place of the tasks you finished.

For some people, a big to-do list under each goal is motivating. For others, it's debilitating. If a long to-do list makes you feel like a weight is being slowly lowered onto your chest, I've got a recommendation: Only look at your list once each week and choose your weekly tasks, making a new, shorter list. Then hide the long list. Only look at the short list. If that still feels heavy, make even shorter, daily lists for yourself.

One trick I teach my students to help them battle becoming overwhelmed in this process is my "just do 3 things each day" formula.

This method increases the chance of continued progress because doing just 3 things each day doesn't feel so daunting. It actually sounds do-able.

Once you've completed 3 things from your list, if you're still feeling motivated, keep going. But if you're spent, then you can relax, or work on something else, knowing that you've accomplished several things that day toward your music career goals.

How do you decide which things to include on you "3 things" list each day? Here are some guidelines: Choose tasks from your bigger, goal-related to-do list that will take from 20 minutes to 2 hours each. Don't choose tiny details, like writing one email or making one phone call as a task. If you have some tiny details, group them into similar tasks. Here are some examples of the types of tasks you should put on your 3-per-day list:

> Respond to fan comments on social media for 20 minutes

> Follow-up on some booking calls for one hour

> Spend one hour working on the lyrics to your latest song

> Re-write your bio for your website and your Electronic Press Kit (EPK)

> Write a short marketing paragraph or two for your concert

> Create a flyer for your House Concerts tour

> Spend an hour researching potential venues in a city where you will be touring in six months

> Contact 10 musicians in your genre and/or geographic area who are a few stages ahead of you. Follow them on social media and see how they engage with fans. Strike up a conversation with a few of them to start building a relationship. Make note of the venues where they're playing so you can check them out for potential shows.

This should give you an idea of the kinds of things that qualify as a "task" in this productivity formula. Now that you have a plan to get things done and build momentum to move through the stages, let's dive into the 5 stages of music career growth.

How to Use The 5-Stage Blueprint

If you're in the *early stages* of a music career, what should you do, and in what order, to make sure you're not wasting time and money on things that won't work for you?

If you're in the *intermediate stages*, what new marketing tactics should you add to expand your fan base to a wider audience beyond your core group of super fans?

When is it time to invest in Public Relations (PR), a radio campaign, or a booking agent or manager so you can make the most of the opportunities that come along?

As I've said, **The Musician's Profit Path** is a plan you can follow so you can make progress every day toward a profitable career as a professional musician.

I developed this **5-Stage Blueprint** from years of trial and error, incorporating what I did right along with adjustments based on all the mistakes I made along my journey to becoming a profitable professional musician. Keep in mind, these are the steps I would follow if I started over from scratch today, knowing what I've learned.

I realize that you may not be solidly in one stage of this plan right now. You may be in a few different stages. For example, you might be in stage one for Marketing and stage two or even three for performing — or vice-versa.

That's okay! The purpose of the **5-Stage Blueprint** is to help you know *what* to do and *when* to do it, and to reveal the important pieces you accidentally (or purposefully) left out along the way. If you have done things out of order, don't worry. Again, this framework is here to help you — not to shame you.

As you read through the blueprint, take note of which stage best describes where you are right now in the areas of marketing/branding, fan-base building, performing and career management. This will help you discover where you can make improvements or course corrections so you can reach your goal of becoming a profitable professional musician faster and easier.

I've included a list of markers at the beginning of each stage that will help you determine whether you fit the criteria for that stage.

Next, I provide detailed explanations of what you can do to move through that stage. One important aspect of each chapter is the discussion of your emotions and mindset. Recognizing your emotions, both good and bad, that you're likely to feel while in each stage is *an important part of the journey.* Many musicians who have followed this framework have told me that the emotional discussion was their favorite part. It helped them feel less awkward and alone when they experienced their emotions.

At the end of each chapter there is a Benchmarks Checklist. Once you think you've reached all the goals outlined in the chapter, go through the checklist and physically check off each box. Checking off a completed task can be so satisfying! After that, move to the next stage.

Are you ready? Let's dive into *The Musician's Profit Path*.

Stage 1: The Foundation

You're In The Foundation Stage When:

✓ You haven't developed a **Mission Statement** and list of **Core Values**

✓ You haven't yet thought through your music's **Brand**

I have ✓ You don't have a completed or well-organized music **Website**

I have ✓ You don't have an artist **Bio**, or it could be refined or updated

I have ✓ You haven't setup at least two branded **Social Media Channels**

I have ✓ You don't have at least 100 subscribers on your **Email List**

I am ✓ You are not **Performing** in public, or you're mostly performing at open mics and coffee shops

Foundation Overview: Build Your Artist Brand Online and On Stage

The *Foundation stage* is exactly what the name suggests: the beginning stage where you clearly know your **Core Values**, your **Brand** and your **Target Audience**. So many artists skip this crucial step!

If you don't do this important ground work, you won't know how to market and promote your music in **Stage Two** and beyond.

During this stage, you'll also create your online platforms that are *branded* to you, based on your music and mission. These platforms will be your hub for communication, both incoming and outgoing, so you can start building your **Fan Base**. This will help improve fan discovery and provide a place for you to nurture your relationship with fans when they discover you.

On the live music side, this is the time to develop your onstage persona and delivery. In order to expect to be paid to perform in Stage Two, practice working towards *being* a great musician, offering entertainment and value to your audience over and above performing the music itself.

Your Focus For The Foundation Stage

1. Establishing Your Artist Brand

Take an inventory of your talents, your experience and your desires. It's really important to know *why* you want to be a professional musician and what exactly you have to offer your fans before you start trying to market yourself.

This personal inventory will help clarify what you want your artist **Brand** to look like.

> ➢ Is your Brand fun and playful, or more serious?
>
> ➢ Do you have any life experience you want to highlight? Have you traveled the world or have a unique cultural heritage? Have you overcome a huge obstacle, such as being a mom, being a single dad, an illness, or the death of a loved one?
>
> ➢ Do you have specific musical training (like at a prestigious school) or are you self-taught?
>
> ➢ Are you bold and "in-your-face" or more understated?
>
> ➢ How will you weave your personal story into your Brand?
>
> ➢ Are you only focused on making great music or do you have an underlying cause

or belief you want your music to be a platform for?

Asking yourself those kinds of specific questions will help you narrow down your Brand Identity. Next, it's time to choose colors, fonts, and a general look and feel. Add some photos that align with your new color and mood scheme.

Next, to understand your brand positioning, examine your current and potential fans.

> What are their demographics? (age, gender, location, etc.)

> What do they like to do? (hobbies, beliefs, causes, types of media they like, including movies, books, magazines and other music artists)

> Where do they hang out? (online and offline)

It is very important to understand as much as possible about your potential fans so you know the best way to reach them, both online and offline. This information will determine which online platforms you choose to focus on and what kind of performing venues you decide to pursue.

If you don't have any fans yet, you probably still have family and friends who enjoy and support your music. Use them as a sample fan base for now. Once you start attracting new fans you can expand your research and sharpen your fan profile.

From here, you'll create your online platforms.

2. Setup Your Branded Website with a Personalized Domain Name

This is the time to "stake your claim" online. It is very important to have a Branded, well-organized **Website** where fans can learn about your music and connect with you.

Only having a page on a shared platform like Facebook or a music site like Reverb Nation, Soundcloud or Bandcamp isn't enough. You don't own those platforms. If you set up shop on "rented land," you'll never know if it will be around tomorrow. Remember MySpace?

You'll want to be in control of your own Domain. Purchase your branded Domain Name so it's easy for fans to *find* you online. Check to see if "yourname.com" or "yournamemusic.com" is available from a Domain Name Registrar like GoDaddy.

For musicians, I always recommend using BandZoogle to quickly and easily build a professional website. Bandzoogle is built by musicians for musicians so it has all the features musicians need, such as streaming and downloadable audio, music and merchandise sales (commission-free), a built-in mailing list and an EPK.

If you sign-up with Bandzoogle, you even get your Domain Name included for ***free*** and they handle all the technical stuff.

Because I'm a preferred partner with Bandzoogle, I've got a special code for you to get a 30-day free trial and 15% off. Just enter promo code WOS15 at checkout.

3. Setup Your YouTube Channel and At Least One Other Social Media Channel for Fan Attraction and Engagement

Now that you've checked the **Website** off of your list, move on to setting up your Social Platforms.

As a musician, you should definitely maintain a **YouTube Channel**. Even if you don't yet have videos to add, you can set it up with your Brand artwork and colors and it will be ready when you start posting videos. After you start live streaming and performing, you'll soon have content to start building your channel and playlists on YouTube.

I recommend that you choose at least one other social media channel and focus on it. To help you decide which one to use, consider:

> ➢ Which platform feels comfortable to you, where you like to hang out?

> ➢ Where do your potential fans hang out (based on your research above)?

Choose one platform and set it up with your Branded images and description. Upload some introductory posts and media so you're ready to start engaging with fans as they visit your page.

4. Setup Your Email List and Get Your First 100 Subscribers

The final asset is to build your Email list. I realize that at this point, you may not have anyone on your list yet. However, during the **Foundation** stage, I want to challenge you to get your first 100 subscribers. I know this might sound daunting, but I promise it is much easier than you think it is!

First, select the email service provider you'll use to collect names and email and send broadcasts. If you have BandZoogle, you're already set. If not, here are some options:

> Mailchimp (free for the first 2,000 subscribers)

> Convertkit (this is what I use. It has many more advanced features you'll want for Stage 3 and beyond such as "tagging," "sequences" and "landing pages")

> GetReponse (includes lots of email newsletter templates and landing pages)

The key here is to pick one and get started. Don't get bogged down with this decision or you'll never start building your list.

Since we're talking about the steps to becoming a professional musician (not an amateur), I think it's important to mention that *looking* professional from the beginning is important. Don't use your regular email account to send out group or blind copy messages. Not only do you look like an amateur, but your emails will probably get flagged as spam and deleted, or worse, blocked.

Now that you've picked an email service provider, it's time to build your list starting with your first 100 subscribers.

1. Reach out to 10 of your friends.

- ➢ Inform them that you're creating an easy way for fans of your music to find out what's going on with you, when and where you're playing a show, when you're releasing new music, and when you'll have a new video.

- ➢ Let them know that you'll also be giving away some cool prizes for your fans.

- ➢ Ask them if it would be okay to include them on the list and ask for their best email address.

- ➢ Reassure them that this is only for purposes of fan updates and that you won't share their information with anyone.

2. Collect those emails in a document or even on a piece of paper (at least for now), until you've set up an email service provider such as the ones listed above.

3. Go through your email contacts, Facebook messages, Twitter, your texts, anywhere you interface with friends on a regular basis. Send the request to 10 at a time until you've reached 100.

4. Now add the emails of any "stray" fans that have followed you over the years and add them too. For example, many artists have collected emails on Reverb Nation or had people buy their music on CD Baby and received email addresses but never consolidated them into one list.

And if you finish the exercise and get to your first 100 subscribers, **Congratulations! You now have a bigger email list than over 50 percent of all Indie Artists** (I researched this)!

5. Perform At Least Once Per Week at Open Mics or Coffee Shops

During the **Foundation stage**, it's necessary to develop your confidence on stage, a stage presence, your attractive artist character and learn how to create rapport with the audience. The best way to achieve this is through regular performances at open mics, coffee shops and small venues.

Many artists expect to get paid to perform right away. While I understand that you may be a skilled musician, getting paid as a performer takes more than skill. A Profitable Professional Musician is not just a player or singer, they are an *Entertainer*.

The skillful performance of a song is just one piece of the puzzle. It's necessary to develop a high degree of comfort on stage. This includes creating connection with your audience, including the ability to banter between songs, capture their attention with engaging stories, and make the show visually interesting by switching up your position and instrumentation,

Open mics and coffee shops are a great testing group for material, both musical and spoken. The responses you get from a "cold" crowd (a room full of people who don't already like your music) will give you valuable intel about:

> ➤ Your set list (choice of song and song order)

> Your stories and visual stage arrangements

> How you can involve the audience more in your show

Once you've performed enough to feel as if these elements are almost automatic, you are ready to start getting paid for your performances. You're ready to move on to house concerts and small venues for pay in Stage 2.

A Friendly Word of Warning

No matter which stage you're in, especially in the **Foundation Stage** , knowing what to avoid, or set aside for later can be even more important than knowing what to work on. When you're starting out, you might be tempted to veer off course by what you see other artists doing, especially those who are 2 or 3 stages ahead of you.

I will probably repeat this several times throughout the 5 stages, but keeping within your own lane and doing the work to move through the stage you're in is crucial. If you do try to jump ahead, there is a 99 percent chance you'll be wasting valuable time and money on things that won't work for you.

To help you keep in check, I'll provide a list of things NOT to focus on, think about or even entertain during the current stage. Your reward for being patient and diligent will be this list getting shorter as you progress through the stages.

What <u>Not</u> To Focus On During The Foundation Stage

During Stage 1, you will be tempted to focus on the following items, because the foundational work you're doing in Stage 1 is a *grind*. You may also see other artists doing these things and think you should do them too. Don't be fooled! These things won't benefit you until you've put all of the **Foundation** principles into action.

> ➢ Fan attraction strategies beyond your first 100 subscribers
>
> ➢ Elaborate Social Media Strategies
>
> ➢ Paid Advertising
>
> ➢ Recording
>
> ➢ Crowdfunding
>
> ➢ Gigs beyond open mics and coffee shops (unless they fall in your lap)
>
> ➢ Pursuing booking agents or a manager
>
> ➢ Investing in PR campaigns or radio promoters

Emotions You Can Expect To Experience During the Foundation Stage

Loneliness: *"No one gets what I'm doing and no one is in my corner."*

It is such a shame that many of the musicians I work with don't have any support from their family or friends, at least, not at first. They are scolded and told that they are chasing a pipe dream. They're encouraged to "get their head out of the clouds" and get back into the real world.

Sometimes, their family and friends placate them with half-hearted support. But they don't really believe that making a career in music is possible. So, when the musician asks for their support and engagement at a gig, or on social media, they suddenly disappear.

Even worse, I've seen family and friends berate musicians for their "silly dreams" and tell them they'll never make it. That can really kill the musician's spirit and introduce lots of fears and doubts.

The best thing you can do when starting out is to find a group of like-minded, supportive musicians to hang out with, either online or offline. *Finding a group like this was a huge factor in my success.* Not only did the women in my group provide support, with praise for my wins, they also provided consolation and redirection for my failed attempts. It was a great place to hear advice from women who were doing exactly what I wanted to do, and doing it successfully.

Having role models can be an invaluable encouragement for a musician in the **Foundation**

Stage because it provides proof that developing a successful career in music is *possible*. It's not an unreasonable goal or a "pipe dream." It can be done, and *is* being done every day by many musicians.

Having a group like this was pivotal to my success. That's why I started the ***Female Indie Musician Community***. It's a group of thousands of women from all over the world working at or toward a career in music. <u>Come join us!</u> – it's Free.

Impatience: *"This is taking too long!"*

Impatience is bound to rear its ugly head at every stage. This stuff is hard work, and it may feel like you've been in **The Foundation** forever. Please try to remember that you are starting to build a few key assets, your identity and skills as an artist, and your fan base. You will build your entire career on the strength of these assets.

A warning from someone who has been there: don't try to jump to the tasks in the next stage without completing *everything* in Stage 1. A solid foundation is just as important to a musician as a college degree is for another profession. So, be fully present in the stage you are in and learn as much as you can while following the steps. It will pay off in big ways down the road.

Overwhelmed: *"I can't possibly do all this!"*

I'm not going to mislead you. It is a lot of work to be a DIY musician. When you start to feel overwhelmed (and I can almost guarantee you will), go back to the section on planning and <u>do just 3 things each day</u>. I promise it will help.

Fear, Doubt and Lack of Confidence: *"I don't think I'm good enough."*

This is completely normal for all new artists. Just having doubts and lacking confidence doesn't mean that you don't have what it takes.

Most artists thrive on feedback from the audience. We feed off of their excitement and enthusiastic response. It makes us want to be better and give them more of what they love onstage. That's why the live performing phase of the **Foundation Stage** is so important.

Your confidence will naturally be built up by the way your audience reacts. If at first you're not getting a fervent response, keep working on your craft. Try to determine whether the lackluster response is due to the structure and content of your songs, your performance ability, your communication of the music on stage, or if it's what you're doing or saying in between songs to keep the momentum going.

Regular performing at non-threatening, non-paying venues can help you hone your skills and your presentation. Keep tinkering with each aspect of your performance until the audience gives you a "thumbs up" by responding with tons of applause, sticking around through the whole set, signing up for your email list and talking with you afterward.

When you've made it to that important level, then you know you're ready to start getting paid to perform. Their feedback will give you the confidence to know you're ready.

Foundation Stage Productivity Check-In: Finding Time To Focus on Music During the Foundation Stage

Often during the **Foundation Stage**, you, the artist, has other jobs and responsibilities beyond your fledgling music career. Whether you work full-time or part-time, outside the home, in your home office or take care of young children or aging adults (which is definitely a full-time job), finding time for music can be a juggling act.

When I first started building my music career, I worked full-time as a Director of Finance for an Opera Company. It was quite a demanding and stressful job, yet I managed to make time for band rehearsals, songwriting and recording my first demo.

When I started to build a name for myself as a solo recording and performing artist, I was a stay-at-home mom with a 2-year-old. In some ways, it was more challenging than balancing music with a corporate job. I didn't get to "clock out" at the end of the day, and I definitely didn't get rewarded with any overtime pay!

Yet during this time, I was able to write and record an entire album, perform locally about six times per month, book several 2-week mini tours, record demos for other songwriters and take a songwriting class.

It definitely wasn't easy for me to find time for music. On the other hand, sometimes the raw power fueled by the passion we have for music can drive us to accomplish the super-human. But passion alone is not enough. It takes battle-tested strategies and detailed *planning* to make sure music doesn't get pushed to the "back burner" when our day job is demanding.

If the idea of "detailed planning" sounds intimidating, I get it. I used to feel overwhelmed by the idea of making plans to get things done. But when I finally admitted to myself that the lack of a plan was what was standing between me and my dream of a music career, I put my fear and resistance aside.

I know you can too! Let me share a few ways you can find time to focus on music while working full-time.

Determine When You Are Most Productive

Discover which time of day you are most inspired, focused and likely to feel motivated to work on music. For me, it is early morning, before the kids are up and the hustle and bustle of the day's responsibilities threatens to distract me. Maybe for you, it's late at night when you've gotten your daily tasks done, or the weekend, when you can devote a larger block of time to music-related creativity or music marketing projects.

We can often squeeze in some short work sprints in the middle of the day, for example, during a lunch hour or while the kids are napping. If you've had your coffee and are in "work mode" that might be your most productive time for music.

Your Lunch Hour: Your Music Power Hour

Whether you shut the door to your office, leave to go sit in your car or find a corner at a local coffee shop, your lunch hour can be a golden opportunity to find time to work on music and make some progress. After all, you're already in work mode and hopefully "in the zone," so, why not extend that productivity to your music?

If you are home, taking care of children or other adults, set your schedule so that they are occupied by a quiet activity or napping at this time so you can have at least an hour to devote to music.

What can you do with these short snippets or time?

1. Work on some lyrics you started writing. Starting from just a spark of inspiration, you can accomplish a lot with a set of lyrics in one hour. You can even use the internet at work for the thesaurus if you get stuck. If you keep your lyric ideas in Google drive, Dropbox, Evernote or your favorite cloud storage service, it will be very easy to pick right up where you left off, no matter where and when you work on your lyrics.

2. Use the internet to research booking opportunities. Choose one method of research each day, such as the newspaper calendar section, similar artist's gig calendars, gigging websites – and focus on that specific kind of research for your lunch hour. This way, you'll have enough time to find some great connections without going down too many internet rabbit trails and wasting time (we've all wasted an entire afternoon this way haven't we?). You may find that you are more efficient when you have a one-hour time limit.

3. Make booking calls or follow up with venues you've already contacted by email. This might be the perfect time to catch them in their office or on email, since it might be their lunch hour too.

4. Bring your instrument or track, and practice in the car or in a remote part of the office. If you're a vocalist, bring some tracks you can sing with or just use your iPod or phone to listen to, review and memorize lyrics and melodies.

5. If you work in a city, try busking on your lunch hour. You might even make some new fans and a little cash while getting some practice time in.

Idle Time Can Be Learning Time

If your job involves a commute (car, subway. train or even plane), there's no need to feel as if that time is wasted. With tons of educational resources online, like podcasts, audio books, courses, and physical books, you could be learning something new each day to advance your career or improve your music.

Subscribe to some podcasts about building a music career so your device will automatically download the episodes. That way, you won't have to use data or be in a wireless environment to learn and be inspired while you're on the go. Some of my favorites are:

➢ DIY Musician Podcast

➢ Bridge The Atlantic

- ➢ Music Industry Blueprint

- ➢ Break The Business

- ➢ Female Entrepreneur Musician *(my show!)*

If you're already enrolled in an online course, take a few minutes at the beginning of your week to download some new modules to your phone, or login to the members area so you can easily access the content when you need it. These extra few minutes of planning ahead will save you time and frustration later.

Invest in Help

If you're working full-time, your time for music can be quite limited. For you, time may actually be a more precious and scarce resource than money. I highly recommend that you invest a small portion of your weekly paycheck into a virtual assistant or local student to help you do some of the music-related tasks that don't necessarily have to be done by you. Ask your new assistant to help you with social media posts, updating your website, managing your email list, writing your email newsletter, writing blog posts and more. Spend *your* valuable time performing, connecting with fans, writing and recording music.

If your day job is taking care of kids or adults at home, save up for some babysitting time. When I recorded my Holiday album, I built babysitting money into the budget so I could hire a college student to watch my girls, then 8 and 2, twice per week for 4-hour sessions so I could get the recording done. It was a really smart investment. Had I not done that, I most certainly wouldn't have gotten the release out on time.

Summing It Up, Goal-Setting and Planning for Success

If you are juggling the demands of a full-time job, try these productivity hacks to carve out some time for music:

> - Choose one hour each day when you'll be most productive and block it off on your calendar. This could be before work, in the evening or during your lunch hour.

> - Use your lunch hour to write, practice, perform or work on booking research and follow-up.

> - Do the prep work for your device podcasts and courses so you can have easy access to lots of audio and written training during your commute.

> - Set aside some of your hard-earned money to invest in an assistant so your lack of time doesn't prevent you from making progress.

If your day job involves taking care of family members:

> - Set aside an hour, either before they get up or after they go to bed, and work on your music.

> - In addition, take note of times when they are napping or doing a quiet activity in the middle of the day and you can sneak some more work or learning time.

> - Listen to audio podcasts, audio books or audio from courses you've purchased while doing

household chores, or in the car while running errands.

> ➤ Set aside some babysitting money or build it into your project budgets.

With just a little planning, you won't have to feel as if work and life are crowding out your music career. You will be surprised at how productive you can be if you deliberately carve out small segments of time for your music.

These time-finding hacks do take a little forethought, preparation and organization, but it will be well worth it. Having a day job might make the road longer, but it doesn't have to completely deter you from reaching your music career goals.

Foundation Stage Benchmark Checklist

☐ I have a list of **Core Values** and a clearly-defined **Mission** for my business as a musician.

☐ I've developed a solid music **Brand** with a unique look and feel including a logo, a font, colors, and other styles.

☐ I've researched my **Target Audience** including demographics and where they hang out online and offline.

☐ I have a branded **Website and Domain Name** that proudly represents me and my music

☐ I have established my **Email List** on my platform of choice and have at least 100 subscribers.

☐ I have set up my branded **YouTube Channel** and at least <u>one other</u> social media platform to interact with fans

☐ I have **Performed** at enough "warm-up" venues to be comfortable and entertaining on stage, and perform with confidence.

Stage 2: The Promotion

You're In The Promotion Stage When:

- ✓ You have an effective, **Branded Music Website**, but not much traffic to it.

- ✓ You have an **Email List** of at least 100 fans but no more than 500.

- ✓ Your **Social Media** channels are established, but you don't have much engagement yet.

- ✓ You've performed enough to be comfortable and **Confident On Stage**, but you haven't yet received consistent pay for your performances.

Promotion Overview: Getting Attention for Your Music and Starting to Build Your Fan Base

Now that you've built your foundation and feel comfortable on stage, you may be thinking that it's time to record an album. Nope.

That's where my advice differs from many other music business coaches. I think investing a lot of money into professionally recording an album at this stage is premature and a recipe for disaster (or at least, disappointment and debt).

The next step is to position yourself (in a marketing way) first before investing in a recording and get a large enough audience to sell it to. At the beginning of Stage 2, when you only have 100 fans on your mailing list, it's a good start, but not enough. It's time to perform at more reputable venues to establish a local fan base, and get a large social following.

Recording a professional CD or record at this stage will most likely result in a garage full of boxes of CDs that you can't sell. Even if you opt for an online-only release, it's better to have people clicking, watching/participating in live streaming and buying to recoup your production costs.

Instead, what I recommend at this stage is to record one really good track to use as an "ethical bribe", or at least to showcase your talent and sound, to build your fan base.

Your Focus For The Promotion Stage

1.Create Your Free Premium Download (Freemium) As an Ethical Bribe to Get New Subscribers

For Stage 2, create something really good to give away so you can expand your fan base beyond your inner circle. This is what I like to call a "Freemium" (Free premium download) and it often comes in the form of one high-quality single or a well-produced live recording.

Freemiums are not limited to tracks, so if you have an idea for something you think your audience would love and be willing to trade their email address for, then run with it. The key is to offer something *exclusive* that no one else can get. This is known as **"gated content."**

Some ideas for your Freemium includes unreleased video content like a live performance or behind-the-scenes footage, an invitation to a private show for fans, contest entry for a prize, or anything else you think would incentivize your potential fans to sign up.

If you're using BandZoogle, they make it very easy to offer your freemium in exchange for an email address (remember, use promo code WOS15 for a discount at sign up). Alternatively, you can use third-party platforms like Noisetrade or Bandcamp, but you'll have to export the email addresses periodically into your email service provider.

2. Promote Your Freemium on Your Website and Social Channels to Grow Your Email List To 500 Subscribers

This isn't called the **Promotion Stage** for nothing! It's time to "promote" that Freemium everywhere you can. Make it a prominent offering on your **website**, add links and posts about it on **social media**, provide the link on **live streams**, and mention it at your **live shows** so you can get in-person signups.

For your online properties, make the Free Offer front and center. Make sure it's visible on *every page* of your website. Make a cover for your social media channels that highlights the free gift.

Live streams are a great place to promote a Freemium because you can easily put the link in the comments so they can click right to it. Perform something live that relates to your Freemium and then tease the audience with their free gift.

One great way to get Freemium signups at live shows is to use a texting app so fans can text a special word to receive their free gift and signup for your email list all on their mobile device. This can be extremely effective if you incorporate it into your live show and demonstrate how to do it from the stage. The social pressure of everyone getting out their phones can definitely increase the number of people who sign up.

I also suggest you create a postcard or flyer to promote your Freemium at your shows. The more ways you can get fans from live shows onto your email list, the more likely you are to continue a relationship with them in the future, and then they can become loyal customers.

3. Get Your Story and Your Music Featured in Local Media

It's time to put your PR hat on. At this stage, it's not necessary to spend money on a PR firm. It's time to build up your platforms and fan base first, before taking proper advantage of that kind of investment. Step up to the plate and become comfortable with pitching your music and your personal story to the media.

I encourage you to start small. Reach out to media outlets in your local area. Call or visit the local paper, magazines with local distribution, local radio stations and cable access TV shows.

Here are some titles of people to contact:

> ➢ Newspaper: Entertainment Editor

> ➢ Radio: Music Director (airplay) or Program Director (interview)

> ➢ TV: Assignment Editor (story) or Producer (for specific show)

If you live in a very small town, there might not be much of a music scene. That's okay. It may be easier to pitch your story with an angle, such as "Home town girl has big dreams" or "Local artist is making a splash online with her music". I also encourage you to pursue media within a 200-mile radius. Even if you live in a really remote area, you can probably find a semi-acclaimed music scene within that range.

Not only will it be easier to get coverage because you have a local-interest story, but this experience will give you an opportunity to become more comfortable talking about yourself in an interview and in a low-pressure environment. Each time, you'll get better at talking about your vision for your music.

PR is definitely an art form and often, not something musicians are comfortable doing. So, start small and build some confidence and momentum. Once you have some local press under your belt, you can use it as "social proof" to land coverage in media outlets with a wider distribution in Stage 3.

4. Send an Email to Your List at Least Twice Per Month.

It's important that you stay "top of mind" with your fledgling fan base so you are developing an ongoing relationship with them. You also want to be the first one they remember when a performance opportunity comes up.

What do you talk to them about every two weeks?

Don't feel as if the task is to write a full newsletter. In fact, I recommend against a long newsletter with several different focuses. First, too many items can divide their focus and keep them from following any of your links or calls-to-action within your email, such as "watch my new video" or "buy concert tickets."

Second, from my experience, when I get a long email newsletter, I usually don't have time to read it, so I put it aside to read for later. Before I know it, it's fallen to the bottom of my inbox and I have forgotten to read it. By the time I get around to reading it, it's old news. If you make your emails "snack-able", your readers will learn that it only takes a minute to read them and then they *will* read them.

Send them one cool, juicy piece of news with one clear call to action such as:

> ➢ Watch my new video

> ➢ Go behind the scenes in the studio

> ➢ Join my live stream

> ➢ Follow me on Spotify

> ➢ Looking for someone to host a house concert

By connecting with them every other week, you are showing them that you have activities going on with your music career regularly. You can create a feeling of excitement for your fans when they are part of something organic that's growing and moving forward.

Writing emails that are short and sweet with a single call-to-action makes it clear what you'd like your fans to do. This avoids the confusion of a long newsletter and shows them exactly how they can support you!

5. Use Live Streaming (Facebook or YouTube Live) to Engage With Fans

How I wish I'd had this opportunity when I was first building my fan base! Live streaming is a golden opportunity to develop a relationship with fans anywhere and at any time. It allows for a level of connection and engagement that is otherwise only possible during a stage performance.

Here are some other benefits that make it such a great promotional opportunity, especially for artists in Stage 2.

> It's Free!

> You don't need any fancy equipment to go "live," just a phone and maybe a good mic.

> Video helps you to establish rapport with your online audiences.

> It's highly shareable.

> You can receive comments live and during the replay, so you can carry on a conversation with your fans.

> You can re-purpose it for your email newsletter and upload it to other social channels for increased exposure.

> The psychology behind its success is "FOMO" or the "Fear of Missing Out" because they might not get another chance to see it, especially with the online engagement of other fans.

> If you're using Facebook Live, you can boost the video as an ad to get even more viewers in your target audience at a low cost.

> You can provide clickable links as calls to action within the comments or description, including where to sign up for your email list, ticket sales and Paypal or Patreon donation links.

> ➤ You can use it as a "teaser" for live shows.

Don't get bogged down by trying to make it perfect. The appeal of live video is that it's real. So be yourself! Obviously, do try your best to create a great experience for your fans, but don't let your desire for a flawless performance stop you from engaging with fans on your live streaming platform of choice.

6. Perform At Small Venues and Low-Paying Gigs

Since you've paid your dues in the **Foundation Stage**, you've earned the right to get paid to perform. Now, you can approach venues with confidence, knowing that you deliver a killer show, and ask to be paid what you're worth.

You may want to try booking yourself as an opening act for other artists. Since you now have a decent local following, you may be able to negotiate a headlining spot at a small local venue. What kind of venues should you approach? Do some research.

First, approach the event as if you were a fan. As a fan yourself of your kind of music, where do *you* like to see shows? Attend some concerts at those venues to see if you'd be a good fit. Talk to the venue owners in person while you're there and offer to send them a electronic press kit (EPK). Introduce yourself to the artists who are performing there. If you like their music, approach them, first as a fan, and start a relationship. But be authentic. Don't befriend them only because you plan to ask them for a favor later. They'll see right through that. But if you are a true fan and support them, perhaps down the road there will be an opportunity to broach the subject of opening for them at a local show.

64

Second, start "stalking" successful artists in your genre. Follow them on social media. Visit their website. Make note of where they are playing. Create a spreadsheet of these potential venues and investigate them systematically.

During Stage 2, you'll get some great experience and hopefully, some new fans by performing at these venues. However, they won't be big money-makers. Most of the time, the amount these venues pay you will barely cover travel expenses, which is why the best route to profit in the **Promotion Stage** is **House Concerts**.

7. Perform Your First Profitable House Concert

I have an entire course that outlines a process called *Profitable House Concerts*. It covers:

> ➤ Booking

> ➤ Marketing

> ➤ Setup

> ➤ Performing

> ➤ Monetizing

It's one of my most popular courses because House Concerts can be one of the most lucrative sources of income for Indie Artists, especially in the early stages of their career.

In the **Promotion Stage**, the best path to booking House Concerts is through your existing fans on your email list and social media channels. Your super fans will be excited to show off your talent to their friends by hosting a House Concert. Start by asking the first 100 subscribers you added to your email list. They are friends, family members and acquaintances who have some investment in you and your career and will probably be thrilled to share your talent with their network of friends.

One of the best things about House Concerts is that the host is generally expected to bring the crowd, so that takes the burden of marketing off of your shoulders. Also, House Concerts provide a performing space that doesn't require high-powered, high-dollar equipment. An artist with no money to invest in gear can still perform a fantastic acoustic House Concert and make good money doing it.

For a full process to produce a profitable house concert, check out my online course here. https://femalemusicianacademy.com/p/profitable-house-concerts

8. Start Getting Gig Referrals from Performances

There is a golden opportunity that most artists are missing. Wherever you perform, don't be afraid to ask for referrals, both from the host and from the audience. Be sure to have a healthy supply of flyers or postcards on your merchandise, or "merch" table that clearly explain the kind of music you perform. Also, include social proof in the form of quotes from venue owners and event planners, and clearly state your contact information both online and in print.

Don't be afraid to mention your materials several times from the stage and ask the audience to take them home to give to friends and influencers they

know who are involved with venues, and
organizations that are looking for musicians.

What Not To Focus On During The Promotion Stage

During Stage 2, you might be tempted to focus on the following items. But beware –build up your business before investing time and money so that these things pay off.

- Fan attraction strategies beyond using your Freemium to get to 500 subscribers.

- Social media automation.

- Blogging.

- Aggressive paid advertising.

- Recording an EP or album.

- Gigs beyond small venues and house concerts.

- Crowdfunding.

- Pursuing Booking or PR Agents, Radio Promoters or Managers.

Emotions You Can Expect To Experience During The Promotion Stage

Vulnerability and Spotlight Fear: "What if they hate my music, or worse, what if no one pays any attention or cares?"

Until now, you've spent your time behind the scenes, building your **Foundation**. You've been able to stay anonymous, working under the radar, setting up platforms and doing a great deal of crucial, big-picture thinking and planning. Even on stage, you were still finding your footing as an artist and testing things out.

Perhaps when you reached out to those first 100 subscribers you felt a little uncomfortable. But those were people who already had a connection to you and were hopefully, generally supportive of your blossoming music career.

Sometimes, asking people you know to support your music can be even harder than approaching the masses. If that's you, and you took the challenge to get your first 100 subscribers, then *congratulations!* You ventured into very uncomfortable territory and now, you are better prepared for what's to come.

During the **Promotion Stage**, you are putting yourself out there in front of complete strangers who don't yet have a connection to you. If you don't take this leap, you won't be able to grow your fan base and advance your career. This step can be daunting for even the most talented and confident artist.

That's because we, as artists, aren't just displaying our music. We are exposing the essence of who we are as a person – our soft underbelly. I know it's a cliché, but we really are baring our souls for everyone to see, through our stage performance, and hear, through our music. Displaying our life's work in the spotlight can make us feel naked, vulnerable and totally freaked-out!

What are you really afraid of? Are you afraid not everyone will like your music? Are you afraid some will even dislike it and be vocal about it?

If you're rational, you'll admit that no artist is everyone's cup of tea. As a music lover, there are musicians you love, some you're indifferent about, and some you strongly dislike. The truth is that the music you dislike still attracts tons of fans who *do* like it (even *love* it). That's because it's polarizing, and the artist know exactly who their fans are and what their potential is. Their music caters to specific, Target Audiences, and they ignore the rest. Damn the haters!

In fact, the worst fate music can suffer is being blah and the worst reaction you can get from listeners is indifference. With that in mind, I suggest that your goal should be to attract at least a few haters. If the idea of attracting haters keeps you up at night, hear me out.

I'd like you to flip this on its head. I want you to think of haters as a badge of honor and here's why: when you put your music in front of any group of people, the number of actual haters will probably be only 1 percent. Therefore, if you can attract a hater, that means you've promoted your music to at least 100 people. That is awesome!

70

Finding one or more haters is just a natural byproduct of putting yourself and your music in front of a lot of potential fans. Promotion is a numbers game. The more you are willing to shine bright light on your music and brave untapped audiences, the more fans you'll add and the more haters too. If you go by the numbers, you gain a ton of new fans *for every hater.* Don't you think that's worth it? I do.

If you're paralyzed by spotlight fear and the possibility of haters and trolls mocking you on social media, I hope you'll try to adopt this new mantra: "Every hater is a badge of honor." If you stay out of the spotlight, you'll protect yourself from haters, but you'll also guarantee that you don't have any future fans to discover you either.

Imposter Syndrome: "I'm not a real musician unless I have a professional recording."

This one is hard to avoid because few artists follow these steps I've explained. Most artists spend money they don't have on a professionally recorded album before building a fan base to sell it to. Since this is so common, you're bound to encounter countless artists who will be incredulous when they find out you don't have a professional album or EP.

Shrug it off! Instead, find your security in the fact that you don't have a pile of boxes in your garage full of CDs you can't sell. Be thankful that you didn't go into debt to create a professional recording.

A quick note to those who have already recorded a professional album (by the research I've done, that's most of you): I have no desire to shame you. In fact, you were just following the popular wisdom and that is not your fault. However, from now on, I hope you are realizing that building a fan base is the first step, not the last.

Impatience: "Why aren't my email list and social media channels blowing up?"

To be honest, the promotion stage is a grind. When you enter this stage, consider thinking about your work on a one-to-one basis. Your job is to win fans, one at a time. This may sound tedious, but it's the most effective way to build a true, supportive, superfan base. This personal investment of building a relationship with each new fan takes time. Accept being okay with that and lean into the process. Don't compare how far you've come to other musicians or be distracted by those who are farther down the road. Keep your eye on the prize and take small steps each day.

Perhaps you've heard about strategies that can cast a wide net online like Facebook ads or viral campaigns. If you think that is what the **Promotion Stage** is about, I'm going to tell you the unpopular truth right now. The **Promotion Stage** is slow growth, consistent progress and continuous investments of time, day after day. Sorry. No shortcuts. On the other hand, there are satisfying rewards. Your fans will not just be statistics, but real people who often become true friends.

Excited, Validated and Connected To Your Fans: "This really is possible and even fun."

I don't want you to think that all the emotions you'll experience during the **Promotion Stage** are downers.

If you're really putting in the work daily, you will see results, and that makes it all worth it.

The best part of the **Promotion Stage** is the relationships you build with fans and other musicians. These connections provide encouragement for you and help you to keep plugging away. Every time a new person you didn't know before tells you how much they love your music, it can make your heart feel like dancing.

Now, you finally have the social proof to show those who didn't support you in Stage 1 that you're making progress, and that following your dream wasn't a ridiculous pipe dream. It is the ultimate rocket fuel!

Promotion Stage Mindset Check-in: How To Stop Playing The Comparison Game

A big danger during the **Promotion Stage** is to play the "comparison game." Falling into this trap can undermine your confidence, mess with your mind and keep you from moving forward.

No matter how well you're doing in your career, you'll always be able to find someone else doing better. In other words, if you let the comparison game and the crippling emotions that accompany it invade your mental space, you may find yourself on an emotional rollercoaster.

Fortunately, there are tools you can use to help you avoid the comparison game and deal with the emotional rollercoaster if you do fall victim to it.

1. Celebrate Your Wins, No Matter How Small

In my community, the Female Musician Academy, we celebrate **wins** each week. I encourage all members to post their wins, no matter how small or inconsequential they might seem at the time.

Celebrating wins, especially when you make them public, can have a profoundly positive effect on your mindset as the wins pile up week after week.

I encourage you to keep a running list of wins on your computer or desk. When you're feeling down, read it over. When you see all those small wins consolidated in one place, they won't feel so small anymore and will give you the strength to push through the hard times.

2. Celebrate Other People's Wins

The other benefit to sharing weekly wins in a group is that you get to *practice honoring* the achievements of others. If you're not happy with your current progress, this can be a tough pill to swallow.

However, learning to be truly happy about the progress of others can be a great character-building exercise. It's also something you can become better at with practice.

At first, you might not feel genuinely happy for their success. Even if feelings of jealousy creep in, congratulate your peers anyway. Over time, if you keep exercising that "praise" muscle, there's a good chance you'll start to truly feel happy for them.

In addition, a little healthy competition is not a bad thing. Seeing what other artists have achieved can offer serious motivation that, with some focus and hard work, helps you do the same.

3. Get Into An Abundance Mindset

Do you believe that every time another artist gets a gig, lands some great press, or gains a fan, that there are now fewer of those opportunities for you? If so, you're battling a scarcity mindset. The flipside of this coin is the *abundance mindset,* where there are always plenty of gigs, press opportunities, fans, and everything else to go around.

Abundance means that there is room for everyone to succeed. Having an abundance mindset can remove a huge burden from your shoulders. You don't have to scramble to get there first or fight for attention with other artists. Your opportunities are out there waiting for you, regardless of what other artists are doing.

Of course, an abundance mindset isn't an invitation to adopt a laissez faire attitude and stop working hard. But if you truly believe in abundance, you can nip comparing yourself to another artist in the bud before it starts.

4. Block Comparison and Shut Down Negative Self Talk FAST

There will always be someone with more knowledge, experience, luck, and/or talent than you have, which is why it's so easy to get caught up in the comparison game.

The first step to blocking comparison is to recognize when you're doing it. When you call it out and put a label on it, you can stop comparison in its tracks before you let it get under your skin or into your head. Notice what it is that triggers you to compare yourself to other musicians and *teach your mind* to react differently. Easier said than done?

First, take note: which situations trigger your insecurity? Perhaps it's reading a certain Facebook feed, going to a particular venue or reading another artist's email newsletter that brings out the green-eyed monster.

There is nothing wrong with any of these things in themselves. But for you, at least for now, your reaction may be undesirable. Once you've built up your arsenal of self-confidence and have more control over your tendency to play the comparison game, then you can experience these situations with a new mindset and see how you handle them.

5. Stay In Your Own Lane

Comparison can be insidious. It can creep in without your knowledge and mess with your head. So, stay aware and be vigilant. The only kind of comparison that is productive is comparing your *then* to your *now*. Make each day or each week a "personal best."

It can be discouraging to see fellow musicians posting amazing, positive and picture-perfect posts on social media. They talk about cool gigs, prestigious awards, top-notch music videos, hit songs or packed venues. It's enough to make even the most accomplished artist play the comparison game.

But they're showing the world only the *results* of their hard work, not the *work* it took to get those results. We don't see their failures, the setbacks, and the not-so-pretty pit stops along the journey to the finish line.

Don't get caught up in comparing your "backstage" to their "frontstage." Stay in your own lane and focus on doing the best you can with what you've been given. A better measure is comparing your *yesterday* with your *today*. Play that kind of comparison game with yourself and you're bound to make consistent progress.

Flipping The Script On The Comparison Game

As you've probably figured out by now, comparison can actually be helpful instead of harmful. It's all in the way you choose to approach it. With an abundance viewpoint and the right mindset, comparison can help you make serious progress in your career. The key is to stay in your own lane and use comparison to raise your personal bar on a periodic basis.

If you can gracefully and wholeheartedly celebrate the accomplishments of your fellow artists, that will make your own wins even more satisfying.

Promotion Stage Benchmark Checklist

☐ I've created my **freemium** and it's bringing in new subscribers.

☐ I am experiencing **fan engagement** through social media posts and live streams.

☐ My email list has hit **500 subscribers.**

☐ I've developed a habit of regularly sending email newsletters to my email list, preferably **twice per month.**

☐ I've been featured in 1 – 3 **local media outlets.**

☐ I'm **performing regularly** at small venues for some pay.

☐ I've performed at least **one profitable house concert.**

Stage 3: The Expansion

You're In The Expansion Stage When:

- ✓ Your social media and website traffic are growing organically.

- ✓ You're starting to get steady engagement on social media.

- ✓ Your email list is over 500 but not bigger than 1,250.

- ✓ You've performed some profitable house concerts and/or smaller gigs for pay.

- ✓ You're starting to get gig referrals and gig swap opportunities from other musicians.

Expansion Overview: Create Lots of Content Both Online and Offline to Engage Fans and Make Money

What is the definition of **content** for a Profitable Musician? Content encompasses all the ways you're showing yourself to the world (online and offline) to either make new fans or engage with existing fans. Use these activities to grow your email list to at least 1,250 during **The Expansion Stage:**

Email newsletters promoting:

> ➢ Blog Posts

> ➢ Live Video

> ➢ Recorded Videos

> ➢ Social Media postings

> ➢ Live Shows

> ➢ House Concerts

Consistently revealing yourself and your music during the **Expansion Stage** is what will allow your fan base and income to grow to the next level.

Your Focus For The Expansion Stage

1. Record your first Album or EP

Yes! It's finally time. This is pretty self-explanatory.

However, let me caution you: remember this is your first album. Don't hire the most expensive producer in Nashville or L.A. Do your homework: look for a reasonably-priced producer who works with artists you respect in your genre. Then, request references and follow-up on them.

Remember that, at this point, you have only 500 people on your email list. You can't expect to run a successful crowdfunding campaign or count on everyone on your list to buy the album. So, be frugal when funding this first project. Consider creating an EP (Extended Play: a musical recording that contains more than a single, but less than a full album). It's a great way to test the support of your fan base without risking too much money.

2. Engage with your fans weekly through email – the SAW Method

My SAW Method for emails in the Expansion Stage stands for:

S: Simple emails with a **Single** focus

A: Authentic communication

W: Weekly consistent emails

I like the acronym SAW, not just for helping me remember the 3 characteristics, but because it paints a picture of "digging in" or getting deeper with fans and making a lasting impression on them through a steady stream of contact. Let's take a closer look at the SAW Method.

Simple Emails with a Single Focus

Most musicians send monthly email newsletters. I am not a fan of monthly newsletters and here's why: when I receive it, I often see that it is too long to read as soon as I open it. I keep it in my inbox, intending to read it later, but life gets busy and it falls to the bottom of my inbox. If I ever see it again, the content is outdated.

Another reason I'm not a fan of long, monthly newsletters is that it divides the focus of the reader. If you have multiple stories or segments in your newsletter, it reduces the importance of all of them. So, when there is a call-to-action in the email newsletter like "listen to my new song" or "buy tickets to my show," it gets lost. The reader ends up not following any of the links and misses out on things they probably would have loved to experience.

Since we're sending emails weekly now, we can focus each communication on **one subject** and **one call-to-action**. Fans will be more responsive in both reading and following calls-to-action in the emails.

If you're wondering what to ask your fans to do, here are some **calls-to-action** for building your emails:

➤ Read a story about you or your music

➤ See pictures from the studio or latest tour

- ➢ Follow or Like you on Social Media

- ➢ Read a blog post on your website

- ➢ Listen to a new track

- ➢ Watch a new video

- ➢ Come to a live show

- ➢ Join you for a live stream

- ➢ Buy merchandise

- ➢ Enter a giveaway

- ➢ Vote for you in a music contest

- ➢ Book you for a private event or house concert

- ➢ Take a survey you created to get to know your fans

- ➢ Respond directly to you to answer a question in the email

These suggestions should help you get started, creating weekly emails that encourage your fans to take action. But remember that you aren't just distributing these requests without any context. For your fans to take action from your emails, they should be moved to do so through Authentic communication and real connection. That's what the "A" in the SAW formula is all about.

Authentic Communication

Even if you don't take any of my other advice about emails, I hope you pay attention to this: *being authentic*, beyond talent and hard work, is the **key** to building a fan base.

There are a few common mistakes I see artists make. The first one is to put on a "Rockstar persona" when writing emails. Resist the temptation to put on airs or try to act or sound like anyone else when writing to your fans. They want to get to know the real you, so don't be afraid to show your humanity through stories and behind-the-scenes material in your emails.

The other mistake artists often make is hiding behind a corporate wall of their own construction. They write their emails from an impersonal perspective, as if their manager were relaying information. They use their name instead of "I" or "me." Their emails are flashy and look as if they came from a label or large company, so there's nothing engaging about them. They serve more as a delivery of information and come across as strictly promotional, not conversational, personal and relationship-minded.

If you have used these tactics because you just didn't know better, or you thought it made you sound cool, changing your approach will develop real relationships with real fans. Instead, be fun and authentic, and let them see your world. Write personal stories that lead them to a call-to-action.

Weekly Consistent Emails

Don't feel sheepish about this! Your fans want to hear from you and want to keep up with what's going on with your music. That is why they are on your list. Just keep it short and relevant every time with a little personality and a *lot of heart.*

Since you've increased your content production, you'll have no trouble coming up with something to talk about each week.

3. Write a blog post on your site at least once per month

Blogs are great for Search Engine Optimization (SEO). As musicians, we tend to have more audio and video content on our website than words. Search engines don't search media, so it's important to have written content on your site. If you do this, your website will get picked up by the search engines and ranked for certain keywords.

Blogs are also highly shareable on social media and will do double-duty, providing ready-made content for each of your weekly emails. A blog is a great place to share news, personal stories and behind-the-song tidbits. A good idea is to put a teaser in your Email with an abbreviated story and then direct them to your website to read more. However, if the story is short, you can post the entire blog in your Email. A blog doesn't have to be long and you can spruce it up with some photos or even video.

Here are some ideas for blog posts:

On The Road

 ➢ Preview an upcoming show

 ➢ Review a recent show

- ➤ Highlights of cities you visited using pictures, stories and videos

- ➤ Behind-the-scenes "reporting" on venues where you performed

Fan-centric Posts

- ➤ Video blog (called Vlog) messages to your fans

- ➤ Interview a superfan of yours. Include pictures or video!

Behind-The-Scenes

- ➤ Stories and pictures from your tour

  - ➤ Stories and pictures from a rehearsal

  - ➤ Stories and pictures from the recording studio

  - ➤ Demo-to-master clips of before and after the process

  - ➤ Story about how a song was written (include link to a free download)

  - ➤ Write a profile on a talented side musician you're using in the studio

  - ➤ Interview or write a story about your producer or mixing engineer

The Musician's Daily Life

- ➤ Talk about your new gear

- ➢ Show off your skills: break down a guitar riff or chord progression

- ➢ Life in the music business (your opinion on specific issues)

Get Personal

- ➢ Personal stories

- ➢ Your philosophy on life and why you love music

- ➢ Family pictures

- ➢ Children's or pet's stories

- ➢ Hobbies or side businesses

- ➢ Your take on current events or politics

Causes

- ➢ Stories, photos and videos about volunteer work you do

- ➢ Highlight a nonprofit you believe in

Other People's Content

- ➢ Talk about other bands that you've played with

- ➢ Review other bands that inspire you

- ➢ Highlight new releases or videos from your favorite bands

- Find a cool YouTube you like (flash mob, virtuoso, etc.), embed it and give your own personal viewpoint or experience with the video

- "Curate" blogs you follow (give proper credit) and describe your own viewpoint on the subject or on the opinions of the author.

- Offer a "guest post" from you to a fan or someone on your team who also blogs

- Read blogs that interest you and write your own completely original viewpoint on that topic

- Create a Top 10 List of the best blog posts on a music-related subject

- After a year, you can re-post an older blog that was popular

4. Use live streaming (Facebook or YouTube live) to REGULARLY engage with fans

You already started live streaming in the **Promotion Stage**. But now, it's best to take it up a notch and live stream consistently at a regular time.

This has 2 benefits:

1. It gives your audience a consistent, specific time they know they can engage with you on a live stream

2. By committing to a regularly-scheduled live stream, you are forced to keep producing content on a weekly basis. There's nothing like a little outside pressure to keep you accountable.

The musicians I work with who really commit to this weekly strategy have continued to grow their audience each week just from live streaming.

Videos from live streaming also make for great email and blog (and vlog) content. Don't forget you can also upload them to YouTube or post them on other social channels. In addition, use them as a teaser for upcoming performances (while getting some practice time in before the show).

5. Expand your PR reach outside of your local area

At this point, you now have a lot of interview experience and a scrapbook of copies from local print media and/or video copies of local online media to show you're newsworthy. It's time to expand your reach. Piggyback off of what you learned working with local media to start approaching regional or national publications.

Also contact music blogs and podcasts where you can get some targeted exposure online. Search for artists who are similar in style to you on Hype Machine to find blogs and podcasts to target.

Before approaching blogs and podcasts, do some in-depth research. Read their blog or listen to their show. Take note of some things that interest you about it or episodes you like so you can reference them in your pitch. The more personal you can make your pitches and the more you make it clear that you value their work, the better response you'll get from the people you contact.

6. Create some social media automation to increase engagement and free up time

The first and most important point here is that I'm not suggesting that you automate ALL of your social media interaction. It's important that you continue engaging with fans on all of your channels.

But there are automation platforms like "Later" that I highly recommend and have used in my own business for years. These platforms make the initial posting on social media much easier and more streamlined.

Try setting aside one hour each Sunday evening or Monday morning to plan your social posts for the week. The platform I mentioned above makes it easy to build a queue of posts so you don't have to come up with everything from scratch each time. Just add some new content to the queue every Sunday to keep it fresh and recycle older posts that got a lot of engagement in the past. This process will make it easier for you to stay on top with your fans, who are on platforms where you've established a presence.

7. Use your network, email list and social media to book regional mini tours that include gig swaps, medium-sized venues and house concerts

Decide where you want to tour. I recommend choosing an area to start that isn't too far from your local area, but just outside where you already have established contacts. Use the techniques I mentioned in the last chapter to research similar artists in the area to build relationships and contact venues where they have played in the past.

Then get one date on the books. This will be your anchor date. You can now start booking other events around that anchor event.

Network with other musicians in artist communities on social media like my <u>Female Indie Musician Community</u> – www.woscommunity.com. Try to meet and get to know people who play in the area you'll be touring. Once you've established a relationship, approach them about a gig swap or if you can open for them.

Contact medium-sized venues and tell them you are coming to town during that particular time window and ask if they would like to book you. Fill in any holes in your schedule with house concerts. Since house concerts are more casual and flexible, based on the host's schedule, see if you can fill in some of your off-evenings like Sunday or Thursday nights. Perhaps suggest matinees on Saturday or Sunday so you can perform two shows in one day. This three-pronged approach (gig-swaps, venues and house concerts) will ensure that your tour is profitable and you'll make the most of your time on the road.

8. Add team members (usually volunteer or barter at this stage) to help with tasks

This one is crucial during Stage 3 and another important reason we call it the **Expansion Stage**. Because you are spending a lot of time performing and creating online content, you'll have little time for

92

the administrative and marketing tasks that still have to be done. It's time to get some help.

The best way to find help is to start with family and friends. There are usually people in your inner circle who would genuinely like to help you and would be willing to do it for free, or in exchange for merchandise, concert tickets or a free house concert. When I was in the **Expansion Stage**, I asked my mom to help me with booking and administrating my email list. Her help was invaluable and she did it for free (thank you, Mom!)!

You can also ask your fans to volunteer for specific tasks on a barter system. Find out if your fans have any special talents like web design, photography skills, graphic design, videography, etc. You might be able to create a win-win situation for both of you where you get their services for free or a reduced price in exchange for helping them promote their business.

If you strike out with those two options, there is probably a savvy high school student or college intern in your neighborhood who can do the marketing and administrative tasks you need at a very reasonable rate. It doesn't matter how you find help, but it's critical that you find it. I can't stress this point enough.

When you find someone to assist you, the next step is to document exactly how you'd like them to do the work and set aside time to train them. It is extremely important to set expectations from the start so the relationship doesn't sour. If you give them guidelines on how to do the work, they'll feel empowered that they can deliver the results you want.

If you don't get help during the **Expansion Stage** and try to do everything yourself, you will most likely burn out before you can reach the career heights and financial benefits of the next two stages. Finding help is one of the keys to avoiding burnout, but there are several other strategies you can put in place to make sure you don't lose steam during this stage which I'll go over in a future section of this chapter.

What Not To Focus On During The Expansion Stage

You have some momentum now which is exciting! But don't jump the gun – keep the following investments off the table until you reach a later stage.

- ➤ Hiring booking agents and managers

- ➤ Investing in PR or radio campaigns

- ➤ Extensive paid advertising

- ➤ Recording beyond your debut album or EP

- ➤ Crowdfunding

- ➤ Online sales automation

Emotions You Can Expect To Experience During The Expansion Stage

Momentum and Motivation: "I'm on a roll!"

If you haven't figured it out already, the **Expansion Stage** is a major turning point in your career. It's that point when the snowball is finally at the top of the hill and starts rolling downward. The slope on the other side is more gradual so you won't feel a huge surge of momentum, but you will feel it.

During **Stage 3**, you'll get excited about the progress you're making, and with it, fuel your motivation to do even more and keep that ball rolling.

Pride: "Yes! It's finally happening!"

There's no more "imposter syndrome." You've recorded your album and it's selling to fans who really like your music. You're playing in some cool venues and have opened for other artists who are at a stage or two ahead of you and you've seen what's possible. You can proudly face your critics and nay-sayers and say, or at least think, "I told you so!"

Valued: "I don't need to settle for being a starving artist."

You've earned it. You paid your dues in the first two stages and you deserve to be paid what you're worth. Your show is *good* and you know it. And now, others are recognizing how good it is by *paying* you like the professional that you are. Back when you were in the first two stages, you may have thought you'd always be playing for tips or for free food and beer.

Congratulations! You've reached a milestone that most Indie musicians don't attain!

Overwhelmed: "The more success I have, the more there is to do."

No matter which stage you're in, it seems as if you can't escape this emotion. Don't worry — it's completely normal. When you started this journey, did you have an idea in your head about what it would be like when you reached this point? Maybe you thought it would be easier.

Dare I use the cliché, *"New level, new devil"*? Every stage has its own set of challenges. During **Stage 3**, it's extremely important that you get help. Your team can keep you from being snowed under by the work needed to keep the momentum you've built going.

There's another cliché that's absolutely appropriate here. *"You've got to spend money to make money."* If you're fortunate, you may find an investor to help you during this stage. But if not, remember that investing time and money in the building of your fan base and maintaining momentum is a smart investment in yourself and your music because that fan base will be a valuable asset for *years to come.*

Expansion Stage Mindset Check-in: How To Avoid Burnout

During the **Expansion Stage**, burnout is a constant threat. You're a solopreneur working hard to expand your music business in every direction. The danger of burnout is always right around the corner.

Feeling overwhelmed, as if there aren't enough hours in the day to get everything done, is quite common with musicians. After all, we are expected not only to perform and record, but also to book our shows, do all the marketing to get people to attend our shows, engage on social media, write songs, keep up with our song catalog and PRO administration, and even more.

Often, artists don't recognize the signs of burnout until it's too late to just "take a break." They end up exhausted, jaded, and many actually give up on music (sometimes until the passion and drive kick back in, but sometimes for good!)

I want to help you recognize the signs of impending burnout so you can avoid it. Once you see the signs, you can refer to the simple changes I've listed in the action steps section to turn it around, helping you to live a healthier, more balanced life *without having to quit music*.

Signs That You're Nearing Burnout

1. Insomnia and Lethargy

Insomnia is having trouble falling asleep and staying asleep. Insomnia can plague people for a variety of reasons, but if you wake up in the middle of the night or out of a deep sleep because your mind can't stop thinking about your to-do list, that's a warning sign that you could be suffering from impending burnout.

Insomnia can become a vicious cycle of not getting enough sleep, followed by feeling tired all day so you're not productive, and then your to-do list grows even more. That will, of course, give your mind more thoughts to race around at night and cause more insomnia. There are ways to quiet your mind and reduce that to-do list.

Lack of Focus or Engagement

A clear sign of burnout is an inability to focus on a single task. Similar to insomnia, if your brain is flooded with things you need to do – after or instead of the thing you're trying to focus on – you'll feel as if you are spinning your wheels. It's almost impossible to gather enough mental power to finish a task with a million other ideas swirling around in your head.

Perhaps you've found yourself trying to have a conversation with a friend or family member, but you're distracted, thinking about your next task. If you can't stay in the present moment and contribute fully to a conversation, it's definitely time to create some mental "white space" using my tips.

When Thinking About Your Music Career Feels "Heavy" (Literally and Figuratively)

Personally, the number one sign that I'm nearing burnout is a feeling of "heaviness" that's hard to describe, but if you've felt it, you know what I mean. Physically, it can manifest itself as a weighty feeling pressing on your chest. Your breathing can feel constricted or shallow. If you're experiencing these physical signs and you don't normally suffer from anxiety, make some immediate changes.

There's also a mental heaviness that's hard to describe. For me, it shows up as a "fight or flight" instinct when I think about having to do certain tasks. I either have the desire to buck my own system and refuse to do it, or I want to find an escape so I don't have to do it.

For example, if I'm feeling overwhelmed by social media, instead of breaking it into 5-minute sessions so it doesn't feel so daunting, my immediate reaction is wanting to quit social media altogether, not even opening the app. In extreme cases, even *looking* at my phone when I'm in social media burnout makes me nauseous.

Sound familiar? Keep reading and I'll give you some antidotes to keep you from suffering these debilitating side effects.

Numbness or Seeking Solace In Addictive Behaviors

In our society, we're never far from mindless escape whenever we want it. If you find yourself sucked into binging on the newest Netflix show or endlessly scrolling the Facebook newsfeed when you should be working on music business tasks, you're definitely using escape as a coping mechanism.

Don't get me wrong, some escapism is good for you. I certainly have my share of go-to entertainment when I want to relax. Just like most things, escapism can be beneficial in moderation.

However, (and I'm going to get real here), I tend to get myself in trouble with a few too many adult beverages. I often have a drink with my husband at the end of a work day to wind down. But when the motive for that cocktail is to shut out the "to-do list voices" in my head or to give myself an excuse for not working on important tasks, that can become an unhealthy pattern.

I've learned to analyze my motives for my desire to have a "happy hour." If I'm relaxing and celebrating a productive day, that's fine. But if I'm doing it to give myself an "out" so I don't have to work on something I need to do, then it's definitely a warning sign that I need to make some changes in the way I'm approaching work so I don't use alcohol as a coping mechanism.

Small Changes That Can Make A Huge Impact Toward Avoiding Burnout

1. Have A Creative Outlet Other Than Music

Having a creative outlet is important. Before you had a music business, your outlet was probably music. But now it's wrapped up in work and your feelings of burnout. It's probably not feeding your soul and providing the joy and relief it once did.

My first recommendation is to find another creative pursuit that isn't tied to goals and aspirations – it's just fun! Take up cooking, painting, knitting, or something on your bucket list.

101

For some, the answer is to find a way to make music fun and casual again to fill that creative void. Take up a new instrument that you're learning just for fun. Play with a jam band in a style that isn't related to your career goals. Explore writing songs in new genres that you think you'll never use in your own career. Taking the pressure off of creating will turn music back into a joyful stress reliever.

2. Take A Vacation

Obvious right? But the key is to take it BEFORE you hit burnout. If you take a short vacation as soon as you notice some signs of burnout, you'll actually be able to enjoy it. You'll refill your empty cup with energy, creativity, and desire to work on music again.

If you wait until you hit burnout to take a vacation, you'll spend the vacation healing and just getting your mental and physical health back to zero. Once, when I took a vacation after already reaching burnout, I spent most of the time playing word games on my phone and looking out at the lake. I wanted to unplug from the world entirely. I was healing which was a great thing, but I wasn't having fun.

If you schedule your vacation to prevent burnout, you'll be able to engage with and enjoy family and friends. You'll be revitalized by doing things you love. You'll come back a strong, whole person again instead of just a fragile shell on the verge of burnout again.

3. Get A Change Of Scenery

If a vacation isn't in your budget, take some time to visit a different location. Try working for a day in a different place – not a different room, but a different building altogether. Visit a co-working space or tackle some administrative tasks at your local coffee shop.

You can also build a change of scenery into your workflow. Start your day with exercise (outside if possible) or take a 30-minute walk after you've gotten some key tasks done.

Try the Pomodoro method and see if it works for you. Work for 25 minutes, then get up and take a break for 5, then start the next Pomodoro. You can use a timer to keep yourself honest. If you feel as if the intervals are too short, try extending them.

Eat lunch in a different location. The compulsion to eat at your desk while working is a common trap for business owners. It creates the illusion that you're multitasking, but you're not really being productive. Instead, it contributes to the feeling that you're working 24/7 and will surely cause burnout soon. Instead, eat lunch at the kitchen table or on your patio. Leave the electronic devices behind! Enjoy silence for a while, read a book or listen to your favorite podcast. Do an activity that makes you feel as if you're attending to your own needs during this break time.

4. Do Just 3 Music Business Tasks Each Day

When I live-streamed a webinar on avoiding burnout, the suggestion that resonated most with the audience was to do just 3 tasks a day for your business. It sounds simple, but there are some nuances to this system.

Choose tasks that will actually move you toward achieving your music career goals. To know exactly which to choose, doing work in advance helps to target those goals and determine their corresponding action steps. If you've put in the time doing this on the front end, deciding on your 3 tasks will be easier. You can accomplish more (and feel the inner reward) when you choose medium-sized tasks. Answering one email or making one phone call is too small. On the other hand, a task like updating your entire song catalog or building your website is obviously too large. Choose tasks you can finish in 20 to 90 minutes each, depending on how much time you have to work on music that day.

If you're seeing and feeling the signs of impending burnout, don't do more than 3 tasks per day. It's important that you hear me and trust me on this one.

If you feel energized to pile on more work after you accomplish your 3 tasks, don't give in to the temptation. Instead, feel satisfied that you were productive, accomplished a lot, and use that energy to plan your 3 tasks for tomorrow. The feelings of productivity and accomplishment will help you fight feeling overwhelmed and help you avoid burnout.

The other powerful effect of the "3 tasks each day" method is that after you've finished your 3 tasks, you can move on to something fun, mindless or creative without feeling guilty! Using this method will quiet the voices in your head. Since you know you'll be getting 3 things done each day no matter what, you can rest assured that your to-do list will be whittled down slowly.

No more worrying, or having distracting mental "tugs" from the to-do list that keep you up at night or make you want to escape. Having a system that works creates momentum in your career and balance in your life. Now, that's a mighty weapon in the battle against burnout!

Expansion Stage Benchmark Checklist

- ☐ I've at least broken even on my first album or EP

- ☐ Fans are responding to my emails, live streams and posts on a regular basis

- ☐ I've setup my social media automation and have been spending an hour each week planning my weekly content

- ☐ I have developed a regular live streaming show and go live on a regular basis at least once per week

- ☐ I have at least 1,250 people on my email list

- ☐ I have at least one team member helping with marketing, social media, booking or administrative tasks

- ☐ I'm getting consistent gig referrals and opportunities such that I rarely have to make "cold calls"

- ☐ I've booked and executed at least one regional mini-tour

Stage 4: Automation

You're In The Automation Stage When:

- ✓ You have an up-to-date email list (dead addresses purged) of between 1,250 to 3,000

- ✓ You've got a living, breathing, engaged and communicative fan base on social media and email who are attending live shows either offline or online

- ✓ You have a system for creating weekly content through email, social media and live streaming and you write ongoing content for your blog

- ✓ You've recorded your first album and have paid off the expense

- ✓ You have at least one team member helping out, whether volunteer, intern or paid assistant.

- ✓ You've executed a successful regional mini-tour and are making consistent money by performing

- ✓ You're getting consistent gig referrals from several different channels and sources

Stage 4 Overview: Create Systems For Attracting Fans and Booking Gigs That You Can Expand into Automated Sales

At this point, you are having a great deal of success, but is it sustainable? That's why, during this stage, you'll grow your email list to 3,000 subscribers and put some systems and automation in place so your new fans will have even more opportunities to get to know you and eventually buy your music and/or merch.

In the **Automation Stage**, you are on the cusp of developing a predictable income as a professional musician. Once you put these strategies in motion, you will be able to confidently say that you are a profitable, professional musician!

Your Focus For The Automation Stage

1. Record your second album or EP and invest in additional merch

Breaking even on your first album is a huge accomplishment – don't discount it! Most musicians don't do that well. Most people who record an album end up with piles of CDs in deep storage. But not you, because you did things in the right order. Hopefully, you broke even *before* selling out of inventory. That means that you can start using the money you're making from that first album to record your second.

Having two albums or products opens up more possibilities for sales. Offering a discounted pricing structure for purchasing more than one product can be very attractive for buyers online or at shows.

Hopefully, you had a great experience recording your first album and can stick with the same producer. If not, as I suggested in the previous stage, do your research. Find a producer who fits your vision, genre and budget who is highly recommended by other artists.

Another way to increase revenue and offerings at your merch table during this stage is to record a homemade album of fan favorites or requests. If you invest some time to learn the best practices for home studio recording and mixing, you'll not only be able to affordably record another album, but you will build valuable skills you can use for years to come to save time and money in the studio. Once you have the files mixed, there are many affordable online services you can use for mastering.

For my second project, I recorded an album of Broadway and Classical songs I sometimes performed at events. Because fans often asked at my merch table if I had these songs recorded, I was simply offering them something they already wanted. I sold this album for a discount compared to my debut album which was recorded professionally. But the most important function of this "homemade" album was to make it possible for bundled pricing. I created a pricing structure of:

- ➢ 1 for $15
- ➢ 2 for $25
- ➢ 3 for $35
- ➢ 4 for $40

Just having more than one album created the desire for my fans to own my whole catalog. This meant that almost every person who came to my merchandise table bought at least 2 CDs.

Since you've built up your fan base to a respectable size, another way to increase overall income from shows is by investing in additional merch like t-shirts, mugs, beer koozies, totes, or whatever appeals to your audience. First, poll your fans to find out which items appeal to them. Bring your fans into the design and creation process. They will enjoy having input and feel more attached to the items when they arrive. This will help to pre-sell the new merch because your fans will have already made a mental investment in them. The leap from that mindset to purchasing the items is not far.

Having more items will give you options for bundling, creating unique gift baskets, and other creative ideas to make more sales.

2. Create a Content Plan so you know how and when to engage with your fans

During **Stages 2 and 3**, you got a lot of practice creating content. Hopefully, you now have a good sense of the kind of content your audience enjoys and what gets them to respond and engage with you.

Not all audiences are the same. Some artists find that their fans love live streaming. People show up at live streams consistently and they participate in them. That can be powerful! But, maybe you've tried live streaming on a consistent basis and you're not getting the kind of response to make it worth your time. That's okay. If you've done a solid test and found that your audience just doesn't prefer that type of content, cut your losses and move on.

The process of creating your Content Plan involves a series of tests. There is no such thing as failure here – you're just gathering data.

Maybe you've found that your fans prefer recorded videos posted on YouTube. Maybe they enjoy your musings on your blog and like to leave comments. Perhaps you get tons of love for your creative photos and short quirky videos on Instagram. Each audience has its own unique way of interacting with the artist they follow.

Creating a Content Plan is like making a good cocktail. Test different ingredients in different amounts until you have the perfect combination. Although the

111

response of your audience is a key component in this equation, there are definitely other factors.

The first factor is your own **ability** and **desire**. Do you enjoy making the kinds of content your audience likes, or does it wear you down? Do you avoid doing it? Be honest with yourself, because there is no point in putting something in your Content Plan if you procrastinate doing it. If this is the case, consider asking someone on your team who might be better suited for creating this content.

Another big consideration is **time**. How long does it take for you to create each kind of content? Is it stealing too much time from other things you should be working on? Does it add too much stress or create too many distractions in your schedule?

Look at the positive side as well – what content do you *love* creating? What really lights you up and sparks your creativity?

After you've taken an honest look at all of these factors, produce a blend of content types, styles and channels that you think will work well together. Create a plan that includes dates, either on a calendar, a day-planner or a productivity app. Specify content types, channels and who's assigned to create each one. Commit to follow this plan for 90 days. Every week, evaluate how it's going. Make small tweaks to make a few improvements.

At the end of 90 days, make time for a full-scale evaluation before deciding what to change for the next 90 days. Most importantly, don't just keep this plan in your head. Write it down or type it up and attach dates to it. I know, sometimes, it feels like an unnecessary step, but I promise it will exponentially increase the chances that you will actually follow through with it.

3. Explore advanced fan-getting tactics like contests and strategic partnerships with other artists

Contests and giveaways can be an exciting way to reward fans for their loyalty. They can also provide a great incentive for people who like your music to take the next step and join your email list.

Whenever I performed at private events, I always included a giveaway at the end of my program. This allowed me to collect email addresses from everyone in attendance who wanted to win. It was a very crude but effective process. I passed out slips of paper to each person with blanks for their name, email and ZIP code. During my last song, I'd ask the audience to fill them out and ask someone to collect them. After the final song, I'd give away a few items from my merch table to random winners I picked out of the mass of folded entries I stuffed into a bowl. The audience loved the experience and I took home hundreds of new email addresses to add to my database.

Contests are a fun way to engage with current fans. Create a karaoke contest for your own songs. Ask fans to send in pictures and video footage they've taken from your shows and reward the best ones with prizes. There are lots of creative ways to reward your fans while simultaneously bringing more attention to your music through promoting your contest and later, announcing the winners.

Strategic partnerships with other artists, either in similar genres or in your geographic area, can be very lucrative when building your fan base, but it's imperative that you approach partnerships with the right mental attitude. You must have an "abundance mindset." In a business sense, having an abundance mindset means that you believe that there are enough resources and plenty of success to share with others.

For example, when introducing your fans to another artist and vice-versa, you are not "giving up" your fans and the other artist isn't "stealing" your fans from you. It's important to remember that we all love hundreds of artists and we are probably superfans of several, not just one. There is plenty of room for your fans to enjoy other artists and for other artist's fans to enjoy *your* music too. I point this out because sometimes, artists get territorial and paranoid about their fan base. If you have those feelings, strategic partnerships are not a good option, at least not until you've developed an abundance mindset. However, with the right mental attitude, you might see the great potential in these partnerships, and use one of these strategies to rapidly grow your fan base.

Strategic partnerships introduce fans to new audiences. There are several ways these "introductions" can be made.

> ➢ You each promote the other's gig or music to your audience

> ➢ You both donate some items and hold a combined giveaway, promoting it to each of your audiences

> You combine forces and promote a combined gig or combined merch bundle to both of your audiences

> You come together with other artists to create a compilation album or joint streaming playlist

Obviously in this venture, it's key that the artist you partner with is as committed to marketing it as you are. In addition, make sure you choose artist partners who have at least as large an email list and following as you have to make it fair for both parties. If everyone is on the same page and does their part, all the artists involved will benefit by raising their profile, getting their music in front of more music lovers, and hopefully, convert some of those people into fans who join their email list and follow them on social media.

4. Book events two to three times per week or book several tours of at least two weeks in length

By now, you're making a good amount of money from your gigs. And if you've been building your network along the way, a lot more gigs are coming to you organically, through referrals and relationships. But don't "rest on your laurels." Keep feeding the pipeline.

Now that you're investing in a second album and some additional merch, you have greater money-making potential at gigs. The more opportunities you have to get people to your merch table, the better off you'll be financially.

During **Stage 4**, consider bringing on additional help for booking. I recommend you find an agent that specializes in a specific area where you'd like to expand – like touring in a particular area or country, or being booked for large festivals. At this stage, you can still certainly do a lot of booking yourself – potentially *all* of it, especially if you've set up a solid system and delegated some of the tasks to team members.

However, Stage 5 is right around the corner. When you reach the **Profession Stage**, it is definitely time to outsource a lot of the booking, so Stage 4 is not too early to put out some feelers and "get your feet wet" by working with booking agents who can get your foot in the door with new, high-profile venues and events.

5. Set up email autoresponders or chat bots to create an "automated marketing and sales system" that goes out to new fans

Marketing and sales automation are extensive subjects. There are whole courses created about them. Although it's not possible to go into lots of detail here about how to set this up, I want to give you some specifics to get your creative writing juices flowing and a **Welcome Email** template to get you started *(see next page).*

The first thing is to determine whether the email service provider you are using is capable of sending automated sequences. At **Stage 4**, you'll need the capability to set up automation rules for "if this happens, then do this" scenarios.

The first automation that is crucial is your **Welcome Email**. You can set this up to send automatically when someone signs up to your list. If you're ahead of the game, you either already have this set up or you've been sending it out manually once per week to new subscribers. On the next page is an example of the type of Welcome email that will help you connect with new fans immediately. This is a template, so be sure to add your own personality to spice up the writing and make it more authentic to you.

Hi [First Name],

I want to personally welcome you to this awesome community and thank

you for signing up!

To thank you for being amazing, here is a free track from my most recent

album. Just click this link and it's yours.

I appreciate that you've given me a place in your inbox and I promise not to

abuse it. I'll only send a short update once per week, always relevant

to my music and I'll NEVER sell or share your email address.

When I am touring in your area, I'll send you a "heads up" (can't wait to meet

117

you in person) and I'll send occasional updates on new musical projects.

Of course, I'll send you more free gifts and exclusive content that only

my dedicated fans get access to (because you're on this list, that's

you :-)

Since you're adding my song to your collection, I thought it would be

fun to tell you a little about myself so you'll know the story behind the artist.

[insert about 4 sentences about you. It doesn't have to be just bio stuff.

You can make it more personal and fun, maybe your likes and dislikes,

what you do for fun, anything quirky and memorable about you.]

I really love getting to know my fans. I'd love to hear about other music you enjoy or your favorite concert experience. I'd also love to hear

any feedback on my music. Just hit "reply" and let me know and I

promise to reply (I read and reply to all my email personally).

I hope you'll connect with me on social media as well. I publish a ton of

fun posts, not just about my music but other bands I like, places I visit on

tour, etc. I like to make it interactive, so leave me a comment or send me

a tweet.

Facebook: [facebook.com/yourfacebook]

Twitter: [twitter.com/yourtwitter]

Instagram: [Instagram.com/yourinsta]

Yours in music,

[your name]

The **Welcome Email** is crucial. After you've personalized yours based on the template on the previous page, create a few more emails in the sequence that will deepen the relationship between you and your new fans.

In those emails, point them to some of your best material, whether it's live streams, videos, blog posts, behind-the-scenes stories with footage, etc. Don't give it to them all at once. As I mentioned in the previous section about writing weekly emails, only focus on **one** theme per email with **one** call-to-action.

I recommend including some compelling stories either about your background, your experiences as an artist or about your songwriting. These more personal stories are what fans crave. They want to feel as if they are getting to know you on an authentic, human level.

Sprinkle throughout the sequence several different calls-to-action including:

> ➢ Connection: Follow me on Instagram or save my song on Spotify.

> ➢ Consumption: Watch my video, read my blog, view my behind-the-scenes pictures.

> ➢ Engagement: Ask them to respond to a question or leave a comment on a post.

> ➢ Purchase: Encourage them to buy an album or a special merch bundle specifically for your fans

Creating a sequence may sound daunting, but once you get to work and start writing, I think you'll find that ideas will start flowing. If you're stuck, check out some of your favorite artists' emails. Ask some close friends about some of their favorite content, either from you or other artists.

After you've created the automation, you'll have an asset working in the background, day in and day out, to help move fans from just learning about your music to becoming superfans – without lifting a finger!

6. Start using Facebook Ads to attract new fans and promote your music and events to existing fans

Facebook ads are a huge "can of worms" that entail pages and pages of detailed information outside the scope of this book. In fact, I created a full course about how musicians should incorporate ads to build their fan base. What I do want to get across here is that it's now time to start setting aside a marketing budget to invest in ads so you can get your music and message out to more new people. Creating a constant stream of new fans is the key to building your reach and growing your email list.

There are only so many people you can meet at gigs or meet tangentially through current fans. That's why you need to get in front of what we call "cold audiences". These are people who have never heard of you before and probably wouldn't ever discover you without advertising.

Some of the most effective ways to connect with potential fans through ads are:

> ➢ Paying to promote a live stream or video to more people

> ➢ Promoting your Freemium with an ad

> ➢ Promoting gigs to a specific demographic

So, start setting aside money each month to spend on ads. Then get educated. Ads have a bit of a learning curve and without proper training, you can very easily and quickly lose your money. Don't invest blindly or ignorantly. Do some research and start small.

7. Create a local and virtual "Street Team" to help you reach more potential fans

A Street Team is a group of fans organized to "hit the streets or information superhighways" to promote you. It's a great way to leverage the fan base you've built to get information out to more people. Fans are usually very happy to help spread the word about your music, either in person or online. They just need direction and specific ways they can contribute.

It's important that you, the artist, are not the one in charge of the Street Team. Find a trusted fan, family member, intern or assistant who is excited about taking on the project. Meet with them to come up with a unified vision. Next, dig deeper to create goals and objectives for the Street Team. Next, plan some ways to start working toward those goals.

During this meeting and the early stages of building the Street Team, develop strategies for asking people to get involved and become committed. Assign tasks to new members that fit their talents and interests.

Give your Street Team Manager lots of latitude to try new ideas, but be sure to remain in the loop. Sometimes these endeavors can take on a life and direction of their own that is not in line with your vision. Clear and continuous lines of communication between you and your Street Team Manager are vital. Remember that the street team is an extension of your brand.

8. Consider bringing on a manager or outsourcing more of the day-to-day activities so you can take on the higher-level management role or perform more often

Although at this stage you may be chomping at the bit to find a manager, I don't necessarily think it's a likely option until you reach the **Profession Stage**. Managers will expect to make 15 to 25 percent of your across-the-board earnings, and at **Stage 4** you may not be making enough yet to be attractive to a working manager. On the other hand, if you are able to hire someone you pay by the hour or on salary who can handle some of the common duties of a manager, it will free up your time and energy for music-related and creative pursuits.

The kinds of tasks you might want to remove from your desk and assign to an acting manager include:

> ➤ Ordering and tracking merchandise

> ➤ Negotiating contracts

> ➤ Managing media relations

> ➤ Seeking licensing opportunities for your music

> ➤ Building relationships with venues and festivals

> ➤ Booking or interacting with booking agents

By **Stage 5**, you may have built up your business to a level that will attract a manager who will accept a percentage, but for now, assigning a liaison to handle some of these time-consuming interactions with venues, vendors and companies can give you the breathing room you need to be more creative and productive in other areas.

9. Try doing a small-budget Crowdfunding campaign to test the waters with your fan base

Until your email list reaches 3,000 fans, I don't recommend running a full Crowdfunding campaign. But I do think that testing the waters with a small-scale campaign makes a lot of sense in **Stage 4**.

There are several benefits to a small Crowdfunding test in **Stage 4**:

> ➤ You get the opportunity to learn how to run a successful crowdfunding campaign while the stakes are low.

> ➤ If you fail, it won't be such a big disappointment or financial hardship.

> ➤ You get to test the financial responsiveness of your audience.

> ➤ You can determine who the best "givers" are so you can focus on them in the next campaign.

124

➢ You get the chance to experience the whole cycle of a campaign. The data you collect can help you improve everything as you scale up.

What should you raise money for in **Stage 4**? One option is to choose a small portion of your second album release budget such as studio costs, your PR campaign and marketing costs, CD design and reproduction, or tour support. Another option is to raise money for a specific project or assets not directly related to your release such as a video, a tour vehicle or sound and stage equipment.

Run the campaign exactly like you would run a full-scale campaign, with just as much focus and effort. Be very specific with your fans about what you're raising the money for and why. After it's over, examine the results to determine what went well and what can be improved for the next time.

Crowdfunding is a huge subject to tackle. I recommend you either buy a book specifically dedicated to Crowdfunding that helps you plan your strategy or that you consult with other artists who have run successful campaigns. My top book recommendation for planning your Crowdfunding campaign is Crowdstart by Ariel Hyatt.

What Not To Focus On During The Automation Stage

You've built a real business now. It's time to establish systems and learn to delegate so you can focus on the things *only you can do*.

> ➢ Administrative tasks: delegate these to team members so you can focus on writing, recording, performing and fan engagement

> ➢ Big budget Crowdfunding campaign

> ➢ Pursuing a record deal (we'll revisit this in **Stage 5**)

Emotions You Can Expect To Experience During The Automation Stage

Massive Confidence: "I'm really making it happen!"

You've come a long way baby! It's easy to forget how far you've come once you've adjusted to your new reality. In your mind, take a trip back to where you were when you started this journey and never take your progress for granted.

Clarity: "I'm unwilling to take gigs that don't pay me what I'm worth."

This is a luxury you've earned. Not many musicians make it this far. Being confident enough in your value to ask for fees you deserve and having the backbone to say "no" if an offer falls short is a strength and skill that you've developed through months and years of hard work.

Once you've been paid what you're worth, it's much easier to ask for it again, and much easier to turn down gigs that don't measure up. As you've leveled up your gigs and your fees, you've created a risk/reward measuring system by which to judge potential opportunities. Whether consciously or subconsciously, you've been adjusting your standards while ascending through the stages.

Stick to your guns. Remember that if you take a gig that doesn't measure up to your risk/reward analysis, you'll regret it. You may end up resenting the gig and yourself for wasting time on it.

Focused: "I know what I am doing, where I'm going and how I'll get there."

You finally feel like a real business owner – an entrepreneur. You've stuck to the blueprint and you're now reaping the rewards. You know that if you follow the steps in **Stage 4** you will reach **Stage 5** and that feels *good*!

Automation Stage Mindset Check-in: Are You Making A Costly Mistake During The Automation Stage?

Back in the early 2000s, I was the lead singer of a successful local band. We performed weekly and would pack the house every week. We were even written up in the local paper a couple of times. A large photo of me donned the cover of the local section of both the Orange County Register and the Irvine Community News within two months. Now, that was cool! :-)

Okay, I'll admit that two write-ups in the local paper didn't make me a Reality TV star, but it did give me a little "status" with my friends and fans. You'd think that would have kept people flocking to our weekly event – even grown our audience. It should have.

But here's where I made a big mistake – I allowed this little moment of "celebrity" to change me. I started looking at myself differently and I started looking at my fans differently. I began to think of myself in a separate category from my fans, a "me vs. them" viewpoint, which was a dangerous line to cross.

It was subtle and I didn't even realize it at first. The problem was that it crept up on me. My fans started treating me differently and in response, I treated them differently. I kept them at arms-length. I thought that I needed to put on some kind of mystique, a "persona" because after all, I was the one on stage and in the paper. They were coming to see me sing. I was "special". Now, I didn't think this consciously, but it was lurking in the back of my mind.

Well, guess what? That invisible wall I created in my mind had a real effect. I stopped talking to people after shows, stopped making connections and joking around with fans, and stopped being accessible before and after events. Did I think I was too good for them? I sure hope not! But it was a subtle mindset shift that crept up on me. And as it seeped in, attendance started dwindling down.

By the time I realized what was happening, it was too late. I'd lost the rapport I built with the regular attendees and because they weren't coming regularly, I couldn't get that relationship back. That was a great lesson for me (and I hope for you).

As a fan, myself, of other artists, I have seen this kind of behavior from them, and it isn't attractive or compelling. It doesn't make me want to connect with them, promote them or support them.

After my mistake, I made sure to keep myself in check. A *new* mindset turned it all around for me. Here are a few of the essential changes I implemented:

> ➢ I became more personal and vulnerable on stage.
> ➢ I expressed my gratitude from the stage at every event.
> ➢ I talked with patrons before and after shows.
> ➢ I responded to all comments and messages online from fans.
> ➢ I always tried to give more than I received.
> ➢ I kept in touch with fans online regularly and gave them exclusive gifts.
> ➢ I never took them for granted.

Most of all, I constantly reminded myself not to think of myself as a "performer" or a "promoter" or a "marketer' or a "saleswoman," but to think like a FAN.

Looking at it from the fan's perspective has helped me create a powerful experience for my fans because I just think, "as a fan, what would I love to see, hear, know, do, receive, experience, etc."

Always remember to think like a fan, especially now that you're in Stage 4 and have a substantial fan base. Never take that for granted. Remember all the hard work and long hours you put in building that fan base.

Your fan base is your asset, just like a bank account or retirement fund. Keep pouring into it and you'll keep earning dividends for years to come.

Automation Stage Benchmark Checklist

☐ My email list has reached 3,000 fans

☐ I've at least broken even on my second album or EP

☐ I have consistent, predictable fans and I have sales coming through my automated systems

☐ I'm spending more time on "big picture" items like planning, writing, recording and performing than I am on administrative tasks

☐ I've tried a small-budget Crowdfunding campaign

Stage 5: The Profession Stage

You're In The Profession Stage When:

- ✓ Your email list reaches more than 3,000 fans

- ✓ You've recorded 2 albums or EPs and broken even financially on both of them

- ✓ You've set up systems using advertising and automation to bring in fans and convert them to customers

- ✓ You have one or several people on your team to help you with different aspects of your business

- ✓ You've dipped your toe into Crowdfunding, but you haven't done a full-scale campaign yet

Profession Stage Overview: You're a Profitable Professional Musician. Now What?

You made it! You're finally a **Profitable Professional Musician**. You're on easy street, right?

Wrong! "New level, new devil," remember? During this stage, there are a lot of decisions for you to make that guarantee the continued health and growth of your music business.

The good news is that you've built your business on a firm foundation and you have an engaged, supportive fan base of more than 3,000 subscribers and even more who follow you on social media. You have the assets in place for continued success.

Here are some ideas to consider, now that you've reached the **Profession Stage**:

> ➢ Should you pursue Crowdfunding or a record label deal? (You may be approached by a label since you've put in the hard work and ascended to the final stage.)

> ➢ How should you expand your team? If you decide to pursue a Crowdfunding campaign, do you need a short-term support team just for that?

> ➢ Should you learn more about sponsorship and try to land corporate sponsors?

➤ Should you start performing at larger venues, corporate events, or keynote presentations that combine music and speaking?

➤ How can you develop relationships with Industry Professionals to increase the opportunities that come your way? Should you look for a manager who can open those doors?

Should you hire a PR Firm, Radio Promoter, Booking Agent, Artist Manager or other consultants?

Your Focus For The Profession Stage

1. Full Crowdfunding Campaign (or Pursuing a Record Deal)

Now that you've reached the **Profession Stage**, you've built up an asset that you can use in two different ways.

1. You can use it to raise money through a Crowdfunding campaign

2. You can use the potential earning power of your fan base to attract a record label

Like any other business, you've reached a critical point in your growth. To scale your business, you either need to leverage the asset you've built to generate cash to invest, or use it to attract investors. A record label is a music business investor.

Now is the time to do some soul-searching. You've built your business from scratch and you've done an amazing job. Are you ready to hand over a large portion of control and income to a third party? Do you even need their help? Can you do better by remaining Independent, taking all the risk but reaping the entire reward?

I can't answer that for you. It's a decision that is different for everyone. Even though I'm a champion for Indies and the "do-it-yourself" model, I'm not going to rule out the possibility that signing with a record label is right for you. Labels can provide connections

136

and large-scale reach that might just break your artist career wide open. Conversely, I've heard many ill-fated label stories from artists about broken promises and misspent marketing budgets.

When deciding, weigh the pros and cons of pursuing a label against what you already learned about Crowdfunding in **Stage 4**. If you did the small budget Crowdfunding test in **Stage 4**, you have some good data on which to base your decision.

> Did you reach your goal?

> How responsive was your audience?

> Do you think they would step up and give more?

> Did you *enjoy* the process?

> Do you have a team to support you?

Whatever you do, don't let this decision immobilize you too long. As I mentioned in the introduction to this book, waiting around for record labels and decision-makers can cause your momentum to grind to a halt.

If there aren't labels showing an interest at this point, that's totally okay. It doesn't mean you did anything wrong. It makes your decision much easier. You've made it this far on your own. You have the know-how, experience and perseverance to keep building your business without a label.

2. Growing Your Team

Since **Stage 3**, you've been slowly building your team. You've added volunteers, Interns, family, friends, and even assistants as needed. But now it's time to be more strategic. The first thing to examine during **Stage 5** is whether it's time to look for a manager. At this stage, you finally have the cache to attract a reputable manager.

Additionally, you may want to look at the roles you have created for your team members and the duties they are assigned. Is there a better way to organize your team? Would it be more efficient and cost-effective to combine several assistants into one full-time employee? If you do obtain a good manager, they can advise you on the structure of your team, which is why I suggested you focus on finding each team member first.

3. Increasing Efficiency to Boost Your Bottom Line

If you do hire a manager, this is definitely an area where they could be extremely helpful. If you don't have a manager, I recommend you take a class or read a good few books about small business accounting and management.

There are two ways to make more money in your business:

1. Earn more income

2. Decrease expenses

If you can find a way to do both of these at the same time, that's even better. However, we usually put all our effort into growing our income in the first 4 Stages. By **Stage 5**, it's time to focus on cutting expenses. Start by doing an audit of everything you're spending money on each month. Are there some recurring charges for software, websites or services you aren't using anymore? Eliminate them.

Look at your team. Are there ways you can make them more efficient? Can you create systems that will allow them to work faster and smarter? Can you swap duties around or combine two jobs into one?

Do a Marketing audit. Is the money you're spending on PR, radio promotion, Facebook ads and other promotion paying off with real income? Sometimes this can be hard to track, but try to identify some indicators of "return on investment" (ROI) and decide which ones are paying off and which you might need to cut. Making these hard decisions is a crucial part of running a business at the **Profession Stage**.

4. Larger Venues and Higher Profile Gigs

The best way to accomplish up-leveling your performance opportunities is to find a booking agent. Booking Agencies spend years developing connections with high profile venues and festivals. They also have a proven system and staff to continuously make contacts and follow up on them.

Now that you're at the **Profession Stage**, it makes sense to subcontract some areas of your business to specialists in order to continue to grow. Booking is definitely one of those areas.

5. Increase the global impact of your releases by investing in PR and radio promotion

This item has been on the "What Not To Focus On" list for every stage since the beginning. That's because it's incredibly tempting to invest in PR and radio promotion before you're ready.

Every musician wants to get exposure for their music and hear their songs on the radio. It's exciting! But as I've said many times throughout this book, it's not a wise investment until you have the foundation set up to take advantage of the exposure, and the fan base to help share and expand the effects of the promotion. Now that you're in **Stage 5**, PR campaigns and radio promotion are good investments.

As I wrote earlier regarding hiring other subcontractors, "Do your homework." Ask your artist community or music mentors for recommendations. These are big investments and will take a chunk out of your marketing budget, so spend it wisely. A great way to raise money to support these marketing efforts is to build them into your Crowdfunding campaign.

6. Diversifying Income Opportunities

This is another area where a manager can be instrumental. Managers either already have, or should be spending time developing relationships with industry professionals, licensing agents, corporate event coordinators, potential sponsors and more.

If you don't have a manager, you can still pursue these opportunities. It will just take some focused time and effort on your part. Here are some potential income streams you might not have explored yet that you can investigate in **Stage 5**:

➢ Licensing for Film and TV

➢ Corporate Events

➢ Keynote Concerts (speaking and music)

➢ Sponsorships

➢ Grants

➢ Session Work

➢ Online Concerts

What Not To Focus On During The Profession Stage

You've finally reached the stage where you can delegate large portions of your business that used to suck your time away from your creative output. At the **Profession Stage**, it's best to be very smart with your time and bring in specialists to handle areas that aren't your forte.

> ➤ Public relations: It's finally time to hire a good PR agent for releases.

> ➤ Outbound booking: It's time to consider hiring a booking agent so you can ascend to bigger venues, book tours and land higher profile gigs.

> ➤ Consider contracting with a manager, but first, do your homework. After all, this business you've built is your *baby*.

Emotions You Can Expect To Experience During The Expansion Stage

Satisfaction: "I've Arrived."

Take some time to celebrate! You haven't just gotten listeners and supporters for your music, you've built a real business. This is pretty uncommon in the DIY music world because most musicians don't have the patience and focus to stick with it this long. You've built a real asset that you can continue to build, grow and nurture for years to come.

Uneasiness: "I'm doing well now, but will it last?"

I want to let you in on a little secret: all business owners feel this way. We marvel at what we've built, but afterward, start feeling insecure about the future. How do we know it wasn't all just luck or a fluke? I'll tell you how – I'm guessing that before you followed this system, not much was happening with your career. If your success can be attributed to luck, why didn't it happen sooner?

Because you followed a step-by-step roadmap to get where you are, you know you can do it again. If somehow you lost all of your fans, your momentum and your relationships, you'd be able to start from scratch and reproduce it again and again because you have a system to follow. So, it definitely isn't a fluke. Rest assured that your success is no accident. You made it happen and you can do it again.

I hope this will bolster your belief in yourself, your business and your future, and give you the courage to keep moving forward without hesitation.

Trepidation: "Where do I go from here and who can I trust with my future?"

As your business grows and your career progresses, you need to rely on more and more people. It's been hard doing everything yourself, but at least you had control and personal integrity in your corner. As your business grows and brings more people into the fold, you have to trust in the motives and integrity of others. That can be scary, especially after hearing plenty of horror stories from other artists, both label and Indie.

The best advice I can give you here is to listen to your intuition, trust your gut, consult a group of trusted advisors (family, friends, mentors or your peer community), and be open but wary.

One of my favorite quotes is, *"What got you here won't get you there."* You've been scrappy and you've bootstrapped your way this far which is a huge accomplishment. However, that's not what's going to get you to the next level. I can't wait to see what that next level looks like for you!

What Stage Are You In?

Now that you understand the complete 5-stage blueprint, what stage are you in right now? These stages are meant to be benchmarks. It is uncommon for an artist to fit perfectly into one stage. If you're a newer Indie artist, you're probably in the Foundation or Promotion Stage, or a little bit of both. For artists in Stages 3 and 4, most find that they have skipped some steps along the way. Following this plan will help to identify exactly where the holes are so you can go back and fill them. If you follow *The Musician's Profit Path* blueprint, you'll not only build a solid career as a professional musician, but a sustainable, profitable one as well.

About The Author

Bree Noble quit her corporate job as a Director of Finance at a U.S. top 15 Opera Company to pursue music. Besides allowing her to use her God-given vocal and songwriting talent, this career shift enabled her to spend more time with her two young daughters.

Bree had a successful 7-year run as a touring singer/songwriter including 3 album releases, several songwriting and artist awards including Best Female Vocalist at the Inland Empire Music Award (2007) and an opportunity to sing the National Anthem at Dodger Stadium in front of 60,000 people.

In 2007, during her time as a touring musician, she founded an online radio station, Women of Substance Radio, to promote quality female artists in all genres. During its 10 years on the air, the station became a highly respected and sought-after source of promotion for female artists, pursued by their PR agents and Record Labels.

The Podcast of the same name launched in 2014 to spotlight quality songs by unsigned female musicians. A few weeks after its debut, it hit #1 in New & Noteworthy in all 3 of it's categories on iTunes and #4 Audio Podcast for all of iTunes. Bree considers it a privilege to discover and promote amazing artists who are not getting the promotion they deserve from traditional media. In July 2017 the show hit 10,000 monthly listeners and continues to grow.

In 2015 Bree launched a second Podcast, the Female Entrepreneur Musician (also #1 in New & Noteworthy). Bree has gathered a wealth of information for Indie musicians through the podcast and other resources at http://www.FEMusician.com.

Bree has created a large, enthusiastic following of female musicians over the years. She made this community official when she opened the Female Indie Musician Community on Facebook in July 2016. The group has attracted thousands of female musicians in all genres from all over the world.

Drawing on her extensive experience as a musician and entrepreneur, Bree has created several online courses to help musicians learn to make a living from their music. Her most popular offering is an online training and mentoring community exclusively for female musicians called the "Female Musician Academy".

Printed in Great
Britain
by Amazon